Coordinating music
across the primary school

THE SUBJECT LEADER'S HANDBOOKS

Series Editor: Mike Harrison, Centre for Primary Education,
School of Education, The University of Manchester,
Oxford Road, Manchester, M13 9DP

Coordinating mathematics across the primary school
Tony Brown

Coordinating English at Key Stage 1
Mick Waters and Tony Martin

Coordinating English at Key Stage 2
Mick Waters and Tony Martin

Coordinating science across the primary school
Lynn D. Newton and Douglas P. Newton

Coordinating information and communications technology across the
primary school
Mike Harrison

Coordinating art across the primary school
Judith Piotrowski, Robert Clements and Ivy Roberts

Coordinating design and technology across the primary school
Alan Cross

Coordinating geography across the primary school
John Halocha

Coordinating history across the primary school
Julie Davies and Jason Redmond

Coordinating music across the primary school
Sarah Hennessy

Coordinating religious education across the primary school
Derek Bastide

Coordinating physical education across the primary school
Carole Raymond

Management skills for SEN coordinators
Sylvia Phillips, Jennifer Goodwin and Rosita Heron

Building a whole school assessment policy
Mike Wintle and Mike Harrison

The curriculum coordinator and the OFSTED inspection
Phil Gadsby and Mike Harrison

Coordinating the curriculum in the smaller primary school
Mick Waters

Coordinating music across the primary school

Sarah Hennessy

UK   Falmer Press, 1 Gunpowder Square, London, EC4A 3DE
USA   Falmer Press, Taylor & Francis Inc., 1900 Frost Road,
        Suite 101, Bristol, PA 19007

First published in 1998

**A catalogue record for this book is available from the
British Library**

ISBN 0 7507 0694 5 paper

**Library of Congress Cataloging-in-Publication Data are
available on request**

Jacket design by Carla Turchini

Typeset in 10/14pt Melior and printed by
Graphicraft Typesetters Ltd., Hong Kong

*Every effort has been made to contact copyright holders
for their permission to reprint material in this book.
The publishers would be grateful to hear from any
copyright holder who is not here acknowledged and
will undertake to rectify any errors or omissions in
future editions of this book.*

Contents

Part one
The role of the music coordinator

Part two
What music coordinators need to know

Part three
Developing whole school policies and schemes of work

Part four
Monitoring for quality

Part five
Resources for learning

CONTENTS

List of figures

Series editor's preface

This book has been prepared for primary teachers charged with the responsibility of acting as the music coordinator for their school. It forms part of a series of new publications that set out to advise such teachers on the complex issues of improving teaching and learning through managing each element of the primary school curriculum.

Why is there a need for such a series? Most authorities recognise, after all, that the quality of primary children's work and learning depends upon the skills of their class teacher, not in the structure of management systems, policy documents or the titles and job descriptions of staff. Many today recognise that school improvement equates directly to the improvement of teaching so surely all tasks, other than imparting subject knowledge, are merely a distraction for the committed primary teacher.

Nothing should take teachers away from their most important role, that is, serving the best interests of the class of children in their care. This book and the others in the series do not wish to diminish that mission. However, the increasing complexity of the primary curriculum and society's expanding expectations, makes it very difficult for the class teacher to keep up to date with every development. Within traditional subject areas there has been an explosion of knowledge and new fields introduced such as science, technology, design, problem solving and health education, not to mention the uses of computers. These are now considered entitlements for primary children. Furthermore, we now expect all children to succeed at these studies, not just the fortunate few. All this has overwhelmed a class teacher system largely unchanged since the inception of primary schools.

Primary class teachers cannot possibly be an expert in every aspect of the curriculum they are required to teach. To whom can they turn for help? It is unrealistic to assume that such support will be available from the headteacher whose responsibilities have grown ever wider since the 1988 Educational Reform Act. Constraints, including additional staff costs, and the loss of benefits from the strength and security of the class teacher system, militate against wholesale adoption of specialist or semi-specialist teaching. Help therefore has to come from exploiting the talents of teachers themselves, in a process of mutual support. Hence primary schools have chosen many and varied systems of consultancy or subject coordination which best suit the needs of their children and the current expertise of the staff.

In fact, curriculum leadership functions in primary schools have increasingly been shared with class teachers through the policy of curriculum coordination for the past twenty years, especially to improve the consistency of work in language and mathematics. Since then each school has developed their own system and the series recognises that the system each reader is part of will be a compromise between the ideal and the possible. Campbell and Neill (1994) show that by 1991 nearly nine out of every ten primary class teachers had such responsibility and the average number of subjects each was between 1.5 and 2.2 (depending on the size of school).

These are the people for whom this series sets out to help to do this part of their work. The books each deal with specific issues whilst at the same time providing an overview of general themes in the management of the subject curriculum. The term *subject leader* is used in an inclusive sense and combines the two major roles that such teachers play when they have responsibility for subjects and aspects of the primary curriculum.

The books each deal with:

> *coordinating* — a role which emphasises: harmonising, bringing together, making links, establishing routines and common practice; and

> *subject leadership* — a role which emphasizes: providing information, offering expertise and direction, guiding the development of the subject, and raising standards.

The purpose of the series is to give practical guidance and support to teachers — in particular what to do and how to do it. They each offer help on the production, development and review of policies and schemes of work; the organisation of resources, and developing strategies for improving the management of the subject curriculum.

Each book in the series contains material that subject managers will welcome and find useful in developing their subject expertise and in tackling problems of enthusing and motivating staff.

Each book has five parts.
1. The review and development of the different roles coordinators and asked to play.
2. Updating subject knowledge and subject pedagogical knowledge.
3. Developing and maintaining policies and schemes of work.
4. Monitoring work within the school to enhance the continuity of teaching and progression in pupil's learning.
5. Resources and contacts.

Although written primarily for teachers who are music coordinators, Sarah Hennessy's book offers practical guidance and many insights for anyone in the school who has a responsibility for the music curriculum. This includes teachers with an overall role in coordinating the whole or key stage curriculum and the deputy head and headteacher.

The book offers many practical hints and useful advice so that coordinators can establish and maintain music as a strong and vibrant feature of the school. It will help readers attempting to develop a whole-school view of children's progress in composing and making music, particularly those who are new to the job or have recently been promoted. This book will help readers develop both the subject expertise they will need and the managerial perspective necessary to enthuse and inform others.

Mike Harrison, Series Editor
January 1998

Introduction

On the whole the quality of music was good. The school was
well equipped even though it was a village school with only one
hundred children. There was no music specialist so a teacher
came in two days a week to carry out all the music activities. The
school seemed to have a positive attitude to music. Planning was
done with class teachers. In each classroom there was a box of
percussion instruments and a tape recorder; tuned percussion was
kept in the library. Music and dance were sometimes combined
and I observed singing and composing.

For curriculum music lessons the school used the Silver Burdett
scheme. I used the scheme and found it had good and bad points.
I found the children did not consider music to be anything other
than this scheme. When I started a lesson with some circle games
one child remarked 'Miss, I thought we were doing *music*, we
should be using the books!'

The school was keen to do music and their music coordinator was
a fairly newly qualified teacher with a lot of good ideas. She ran
workshops for the other teachers.

Music was not taught by class teachers but by the music
coordinator. Lessons were fortnightly and lasted 45 minutes.

This school followed the BBC music programmes and by the time the children were in Y6 they were fed up with the format. Their resources were poor and there was no music specialist to fight for the subject. If I compare this school to my local school at home one can see how different things are: it is fairly well off and they make a point of funding music. This is partly due to the fact that half the teachers are very enthusiastic about the subject. Music is taught very well and it has got through to the majority of children.

(Student teachers' observations of music in primary schools where they are placed for a 10–week teaching practice)

These are snapshots, taken in 1996, of provision and practice in a number of primary schools in England, all of which have the National Curriculum in place. What is evident is that the type, quantity and quality of provision is still hugely varied. The feature that seems to make the most positive impact is the presence of a teacher or teachers who have enthusiasm and confidence to be involved in teaching music and to make sure that it is valued by the school community.

It is these qualities of confidence and enthusiasm, as well as a creative approach to teaching, which are the hallmarks of good practice.

Evidence of music's status in a school is usually easily come by:

- music written into the timetable for every class (not last thing on a Friday),
- good quality singing in assembly,
- children learning instruments,
- opportunities for elective music-making (choir, recorder groups, steel band etc.),
- good quality, well-maintained instruments for the classroom,
- music corners or workstations in classrooms,
- a variety of teaching resources,
- the inclusion of music in the planning for cross-curricular work.

All of these and others will be the result of the energy, thought and commitment of a teacher or teachers who have set out to establish and maintain music as a strong and vibrant feature of the school's curriculum. The arts, perhaps more than other subjects, rely very much on the particular individual teacher's approach and attitude. They have to be constantly fought for in primary schools, unlike maths, for instance, which would never be marginalised and neglected because of a lack of teachers' recognition of its importance. They are subjects that need to be animated and modelled through practice, otherwise the child will be only a consumer and spectator of the work of others.

Where music in the curriculum is reliant on the input of a visiting specialist who has little opportunity to discuss her work with staff or be involved in planning with reference to other curriculum areas, it is difficult to see ways in which the quality and status of music can be improved or developed. For small schools the problem of subject expertise amongst (or between) full-time staff may remain a problem; however if it is recognised that any part-time specialist teaching needs to be integrated with the rest of the curriculum, the problem of isolation may be overcome. There need to be opportunities for some exchange of teaching ideas and joint planning. This will serve not only the purpose of connecting music with other related learning but also offer the possibility of the full-time teachers developing their own understanding and involvement in the music curriculum.

The HMI review *The Teaching and Learning of Music* (1991) summarised findings from inspections of 285 primary schools in England carried out between 1982 and 1989. This was a period of enormous upheaval in schools, when the working conditions of teachers changed and all aspects of curriculum content, educational aims and approaches to assessment were under scrutiny from the government, the media and the profession itself.

The review comments that

 music-making of quality was better developed where there was at least one teacher with sufficient expertise in the subject to give curriculum leadership in the school.
. . . the work of the specialist music teachers could be somewhat isolated from the rest of the curriculum which indicated a need for thorough consultation between specialist and classteachers.

Three distinct but overlapping roles were identified amongst the specialist teachers:

> *First, although most had a class teaching responsibility, they also taught music to classes other than their own. Successful work depended on the amount of time allocated to these lessons and the teacher's ability to provide a range of appropriate musical activities. Second, teachers with particular expertise made valuable contributions to the extra curricular work . . . high standards were regularly achieved which could greatly enrich the work in school hours. Third, but less frequently, teachers with specialist expertise supported their colleagues by preparing guidelines, helping with the selection of appropriate teaching materials, offering advice about teaching . . . and, in a small number of cases, providing more focused in-service training for the whole staff or groups of teachers.*

The following published review of findings for 1993/94 (OFSTED) raised the same issue. The report recommended that 'primary schools need to continue to develop the role of coordinators and, where possible, provide the time for them to work effectively with class teachers who need their support'.

Most recently Janet Mills, HMI, reports in *Primary Music Today* (May 1997) that in inspections carried out in 1995/96,

> *The schools where attainment is high have usually invested wisely in the systematic development of teachers' abilities to teach music. . . . There is no evidence of a general link between 'specialist' teaching and the quality with which class music is taught in Key Stage 1 or Key Stage 2.*

The music coordinator who recognises the importance of an inclusive approach to teaching music will need to demonstrate this not only in what and how music is taught, but who teaches it. The role of coordinator needs to encompass not only those skills associated with music itself but also skills which are concerned with
- effective communication,
- managing change in professional attitudes and practices,
- advising and supporting colleagues,
- being the advocate for music in the school community.

When music is well established in a school as an integral part of children's experience; where there are regular, ordinary occasions when children can share their music making, there is likely to be a well developed sense of community. Music celebrates, stimulates, soothes, comforts, challenges, and unites the human mind and spirit.

Its role as a means of offering therapy in the field of special needs is now well-recognised and established and we should not forget, in the hurly-burly of life in the primary school, that music offers all of us moments of sheer pleasure and enjoyment.

Music teachers themselves are often so preoccupied with the mechanics of making music happen that they may neglect, even forget these fundamental reasons for their own, let alone anyone else's, involvement in the subject. When saying 'farewell' to yet another batch of newly qualified specialist music teachers I always urge them to remember their own needs as musicians — to look for opportunities for participating in music-making of all kinds; to learn a new skill, to join or form a choir/band/orchestra, to compose and arrange. Teaching in primary school can easily consume most of your mental and physical energy but keeping some to expend on yourself can be refreshing and rewarding. Good teachers need to be good learners; motivated to continue to look for new ideas in order to develop and challenge their professional practice.

This book does not set out to offer a blueprint for how music coordinators should function. It is concerned with raising issues and questions, offering examples of good or typical practice, providing advice and information and, on occasion, suggesting solutions to some common problems. Much of the content is drawn from research carried out through interviews with, and small-scale surveys of serving teachers whom I have worked with on inservice courses. They have been generous not only with their time, but also in providing me with examples of their planning materials.

I would like to acknowledge the cooperation and advice given by Rob Bennett, Louise Hankin, Julie Janota, Philip Marples,

Yvonne Renouf, Wendy Reynolds, Daphne Shaw, Tony Wade and Clare Wilson, and all the music coordinators who have attended GEST-funded courses in Devon and Cornwall.

Noelle Boucherat, Derek Kitt, Chris Naughton and Anice Paterson, have also offered invaluable advice and acted as sounding boards for my ideas, to them many thanks.

Part one | The role of the music coordinator

Chapter 1
The role of the music
coordinator

Chapter 2
Consultancy

Chapter 1   The role of the music coordinator

The job description

In advertisements and job descriptions the title given to the teacher responsible for music in a primary school may vary and the particular one that is chosen is likely to suggest the school's previous experience or expectations of the post.

'Music specialist' implies a teacher with traditional expertise who may be expected to teach music to all or most of the children. This kind of post has become increasingly rare in state education for a combination of reasons both economic and philosophical. What is not rare is the 'fall-out' from this title which continues to lead teachers to believe that music can only be the province of specialist teachers. Music is seen as a special specialism: a subject that teachers can, quite openly and without shame, admit to not teaching.

A teacher **'able to offer music'** suggests a more flexible and negotiable situation. It does not imply a post of responsibility and there may be other teachers already working in the school who have expertise. They may be looking for someone to strengthen the provision in some way. What this phrase suggests, perhaps, is that the school recognises that no single specialist can provide the full range of expertise or interests which a curriculum subject needs.

A teacher **'to take responsibility for music'** is a little vague whereas **'curriculum leader'** or **'co-ordinator'** suggests that the school has clear expectations and gives similar status to music as it does to other subjects.

However, in practice, these titles are sometimes used interchangeably. It is therefore very important that at interview or, in the early stages of a new appointment, expectations of responsibilities are articulated and agreed.

Expectations of schools

It is evident, from job descriptions in the press and the more detailed information that applicants receive from schools, that expectations of such a post vary widely. The status given to the post can initially be gleaned from whether it attracts a responsibility allowance. In comparing similar sized schools there is no guarantee of the post carrying the same allowance as individual schools will decide on where to spend their budget according to the particular interests, philosophy and enthusiasms of the management.

Heads and governors, when appointing a teacher to take on responsibility for music, may well be influenced by their own experience of school music. Job descriptions are often loaded with expectations about what kinds of musical activities are desirable, or are to be promoted. The headteacher's definition of a music specialist and consequently, what kind of music education s/he is prepared to support is highly significant and can greatly facilitate or hinder the aims of the coordinator.

The other significant influence on a job description is whom you might be replacing. Where a school has lost a teacher responsible for music who was in post for a considerable time, the subject is likely to have developed as a close reflection of his/her strengths and values. The musical activity in the school will have a particular expression which, if the management approves, they will want to continue. If, for instance, a school has an excellent tradition of singing with a choir that performs at festivals, or a large number of children learning instruments, or a tradition of combined arts projects, then it may well want to find a teacher who will continue in the same mould. On the other hand, a school might be appointing a coordinator for the first time, having survived, say, on generalist teaching supported by a bought-in specialist. In this case they may well not know quite what they want, or what is possible. Indeed, they may have a very limited view of the role (i.e. pianist).

These are extracts from a sample of job descriptions provided for applicants in recent years:

Music Coordinator — Rate B Allowance
Alongside the headteacher, take the lead in the planning and development of the music curriculum throughout, the school . . .
Assessing the needs of the school in terms of music resources and equipment . . .
Assessing INSET needs of the school and taking a lead in planning and organising school based courses . . .
Providing general guidance to staff . . .
Developing liaison with LEA services and other agencies
Overseeing the work of visiting peripatetic teachers
Select suitable children for instrumental tuition
Assist with administration of the music budget
Be responsible for collecting fees for tuition and maintenance of instruments

You will obviously need the ability to be flexible and be able to play an instrument (ideally the piano) to support specific activities e.g. assembly/concerts/orchestra work/making music.

Ability to lead choir and orchestra essential.

training instrumental groups, recorder groups and the orchestra; training and accompanying the choir, planning, teaching and accompanying music for assembly (No mention in this one of curriculum work at all).

the music specialist will be required to deliver the National Curriculum and music to all ages from nursery to Y6, as well as liaise with class teachers, clergy and visiting peripatetics. S/he will also be responsible for church and school assemblies and productions.

The degree of detail provided and the kind of responsibilities described reveal some marked differences in what is envisaged. Apart from the first extract all the others emphasise the skills of a musical director rather than a teacher of curriculum music.

Although these kinds of descriptions indicate a view or preference it may not mean that a broader and more comprehensive approach is unwelcome. It should signal the need for educating the headteacher and perhaps the school as a whole in other kinds of music learning. It may also suggest a 'softly-softly' approach to change and development; during the first months of teaching one should attempt to provide a certain amount of what is expected, especially where traditions are in place. Change and innovation should be approached with awareness of the difficulties colleagues may have with altering their attitudes and accommodating your ideas.

Recent developments in the coordinator role

The word 'coordination' suggests that there are people or things to be brought together and organised in some purposeful way. Often with music there has been little need to do this as most of the teaching and activity has emanated from one member of staff: the music 'specialist'. Coordination related more to the business of organising peripatetic instrumental teaching and extra-curricular music activities. Until the mid 70s most average to large primary schools could, if they chose, afford to employ a music teacher to do nothing but teach music throughout the school or, at least spend a substantial amount of their weekly timetable on this, perhaps sharing a class-teacher post for the remainder. This policy meant that, for smaller schools, there was no need for a full-time music teacher and someone could be employed for, perhaps, one day per week to teach each class and take some recorder groups or the choir. Some local education authorities even paid for pianists who were not qualified school teachers, to work as accompanists in school; the assumption being, I imagine, that without a pianist no music was possible, or that pianist equals music teacher. Where there was no specialist, the visiting pianist could end up leading music lessons. This might have

Music is for all children therefore it should be
taught by all teachers.   (Mills, 1991)

...the responsibility for the development of
the child through a musical education does not
rest with one person.
                              (Nelson in Glover and Ward, 1993)

appeared to be better than nothing but it is interesting that the
criteria for being able to teach music are considered to be
rather different from those required to teach other subjects.

Now that staffing patterns have changed due largely, I suspect,
to economics rather than ideology, it is less possible for
schools to find the means to employ a music teacher who
operates as a specialist throughout the school. Alongside this
resource issue there have also been changes in attitudes and
thinking towards music in primary schools.

With most curriculum subjects in primary school one assumes
that teachers are engaged with teaching them to their own
class. One may also assume that these teachers accept that this
is what characterises the job of a primary class teacher. When I
interview candidates for initial teacher training a major reason
for choosing to teach in the primary phase is their interest in
the whole child and wanting to be involved with the whole
curriculum. They may express lack of experience or knowledge
with some subjects but they still expect to be teaching them.
This does not deny the fact that we all have differing degrees
of knowledge, skill and understanding in different subjects or
that we enjoy teaching some subjects more than others.

The principle of the class teacher teaching all subjects
to the same group of children throughout a year is deeply
embedded in theory and practice, except for music, and the way
in which many specialist music teachers have been educated
perpetuates this perception. The popular image of the music
teacher is still of an accomplished performer (invariably a
pianist) of 'classical' music. S/he understands the mysteries
of staff notation and will devote much energy and time to
directing choirs, ensembles and providing a regular stream of
concerts and performance events to uphold (or establish) the
school's traditions. The problem with this image is that it is at
odds with much of what is now considered to be appropriate
and desirable for curriculum music in school. In the current
climate improvising, composing, listening and responding are
all considered, with performing, to be integral to the music
education of all children. However it is expressed, the
curriculum documents for music in all four countries in the
UK ask for these activities to be the means by which children

learn in and through music. The teaching and learning styles needed for the contemporary curriculum encompass those associated with other subjects: facilitating, guiding, peer teaching, group work, independent learning, self-assessment. None of these feature very much in the music education traditions of even the quite recent past. Music teachers who have been educated through 'O' and 'A' levels and a predominantly 'classical' music route will be more familiar with the 'teacher as musical director/instructor' model of teaching. Generalist teachers who were on the receiving end of this approach will assume that this is what music teaching is. If it is, then of course there is no possibility that they could do it!

Teachers who are accomplished (often self-taught) guitar players, singers, drummers etc. seem to think that, because they have had no formal music education and do not read music, they cannot or should not teach music. Ironically, it is often these teachers who have the abilities to play by ear, improvise and who are comfortable with pop, folk or jazz styles. Current views of curriculum content and teaching styles encompass all of this, and teachers who have had a 'classical' music education may be less confident in such skills and knowledge.

Now that teaching music calls on a greater range of teaching skills and musical activities, coordinators must work hard to promote and demonstrate music as a subject that all good teachers can teach; and exploit the enthusiasms and skills of colleagues.

As long as primary schools continue to uphold the principle of the class teacher teaching the whole curriculum, music coordinators need to address the problems of the confidence and expertise of colleagues. Confidence develops as a result of positive experience leading to greater understanding of what music is, how children learn and what can be taught. Expertise is developed through the acquisition of skills in and knowledge of music itself.

The problem increases, quite understandably, as the children become more experienced and more critical themselves. There are few who would argue that a specialist teacher is necessary to teach at KS1; the nature of children's musical abilities, understanding and engagement at this stage means that all teachers should be able to handle the appropriate musical skills and knowledge. They will, of course, still need the support and advice of a coordinator but I have found, in my own experience of providing inservice courses, that KS1 teachers are generally convinced of the importance of music in the education of young children, and confident to 'have a go'.

In Years 3 and 4 it should still be perfectly possible for the majority of teachers to be teaching music to their own classes, but it is in Years 5 and 6 that teachers may begin to be anxious about their own subject knowledge and their abilities to provide musical experiences that are complex and challenging enough to allow for progression. At this stage the music coordinator may well be expected to teach as a specialist. There are many instances of teachers swapping classes to teach their subject specialism, especially in Year 6, and in music it is extremely common. In 1995 I carried out a survey of teachers who were in their first three years of teaching (all graduates of the BAEd and PGCE specialist primary music courses at Exeter University). Out of 36 respondents 33 were responsible for music throughout their school and 10 cited teaching some or most other classes for music as one of their responsibilities. More recently I have been collecting data from fifteen teachers involved in an inservice course specifically for music coordinators (a government-funded course run jointly with Cornwall Education Authority) and half the respondents teach other's classes as part of their role. It may be that this pattern is the most effective and appropriate, but the decision about who teaches what should be made as a result of a period of review and reflection rather than a situation arrived at by default, inertia, desperation or ignorance.

Responsibilities

In all the interviews and questionnaires that I have undertaken there is a common core of responsibilities which all coordinators take on where relevant:

1   Purchasing and maintaining music resources. These include sheet music, published teaching materials, instruments, recorded music, music stands and storage;
2   Accompanying the singing in assembly and taking singing practices, although other teachers might contribute;
3   Organising instrumental tuition provided by visiting teachers;
4   Directing and teaching several performance groups such as recorders, choir, orchestra, steel band, guitars, keyboard. These usually take place during lunch-times or after school;
5   Directing or contributing significantly to performance events attached to religious festivals, and end of term celebrations; concerts, and music making with other schools;
6   Organising visits to concerts or visits by musicians to the school;
7   Writing the policy document for the school;
8   Bidding for money and managing the budget;
9   Taking responsibility for curriculum development;
10 Providing advice and support for colleagues. (This ranged from writing detailed lesson plans for other teachers, to devising a series of INSET sessions with the whole staff, to acting mainly in the role of consultant to one or more teachers);
11 Developing a framework and guidelines for assessment;
12 Dealing with music related correspondence;
13 Attending meetings and courses relevant to own professional development.

(I have identified a further responsibility which was not mentioned by respondents to questionnaires and that is the task of liaising with feeder schools and the secondary school/s).

These responsibilities varied greatly in relation to the size of the school, the extent of activity which had been established and how much other teachers were involved. For instance, some large schools might have six or more different instrumental teachers visiting the school every week, others may have none. However, from all respondents there was a clear recognition that the character, status and amount of music-related activity in the school was very much a reflection of their personal contribution.

Clare, in her first job after qualifying faced immediate specialist responsibilities:

I said in my interview that I would want my main focus, especially to begin with, to be my class, and the school is happy with this. So it hasn't been crash, bang right from the start but to all intents and purposes I am the music coordinator. I mean, from day one all the music post was put in my pigeon hole and it has to be dealt with. And people saying 'recorder groups' ... so you have to do it. They might say 'you can get into it gently' but on a practical, day to day basis there are certain things that just have to happen like sorting out recorder groups and ordering resources and playing for assembly. Choir has to start right away and planning, which I've done for my phase group which is Year 3/4. The other phases do their own at the moment.

Points 1 to 6 in the list are self-explanatory, familiar and traditional music specialist responsibilities. (I will deal with these in later sections): aspects of the job which, if already established, have to be taken on straight away.

Where there is a lot of extra curricular music-making established that you are expected to continue, then you need to allow yourself the time to get the measure of it and delay attempting to change or introduce new ventures for quite some time, probably a full academic year. However, you may need to tackle some things straight away, just to make your work easier.

Again, Clare found that she had to do this:

One of the things I found really difficult when I started was that colleagues were giving me things to play in assembly with two minutes notice and expecting me to be able to play it straight off. So I spent about half a day going through all the songs that are commonly used for assemblies, sorting them into folders and I put up a complete list in the staff room. The idea being that when a class teacher plans their assembly they can choose the song they want and tell me days in advance. That's just one little thing.

In the next staff meeting I'm going to explain to everyone why I've done this and that I need time to prepare.

What else ... I've changed the choir. They had a choir of about 30 to 40 but towards the end of last half term it was up to 60 so I've split it into a choir and a training choir. And a part-time teacher who is also a music specialist is taking the training choir.

Where there are other teachers with music expertise you should encourage their involvement particularly with extra-curricular activity.

The rest of the list might appear in the description for coordinating any subject although point 10 could be a particularly significant part of your role depending on the quality and quantity of music teaching throughout the school. These responsibilities will be dealt with in this section.

Theory and practice

As the music coordinator you must be clear about your own professionalism.

You need to reflect on your own theory and practice before offering them as a model or promoting them as the foundations for curriculum policy and development. If you are newly qualified or in the early years of teaching experience you may find this reflection an activity you are familiar with. During training and initial teaching experience you will have become used to evaluating and discussing your learning and your practice; and developing your personal philosophy as a teacher.

On the other hand, if you have been teaching for some years the need to think about and articulate your own principles may well have faded into the background. Music teachers have traditionally not been used to articulating the theory that forms the basis of their practice: the justifications for teaching music have seemed so obvious and uncontentious that debate about why we teach music and the value of what is taught has been rather thin on the ground.

Music teachers, perhaps more so than the teachers of other arts subjects have been preoccupied with product: generating performances, passing on techniques and knowledge to facilitate performance and, when there is time, encouraging appreciative listening. If children are seen and heard to be engaged in performing music then surely this is its own justification? The debate generated by the introduction of the National Curriculum for music was refreshing and energising. It demanded that music teachers articulated their views to other teachers and the public in a way that has perhaps never been required before. The climate in the profession now expects us to be accountable, coherent and convincing in our rationale and our aims for teaching music. Despite the apparent status that music now has in schools as a legal requirement, there continues to be the need for music teachers to argue and lobby for it. We have to convince colleagues, parents and management that music is more than a leisure pursuit, an activity for the talented few, just good fun, a luxury to be enjoyed after 'real' work has been finished, or window dressing. Some of these attitudes are manifested in schools in quite obvious ways:

- music timetabled for Friday afternoon, but sometimes does not happen because work needs to be finished off,
- when there is disruption to the timetable for some special project or event it is music (or other arts subjects) which is abandoned,
- resourcing is channelled into productions rather than into the needs of curriculum music,
- auditioning and selection for extra-curricular music activities.

These are just four examples and the last one might well be justifiable in certain circumstances but the priority in primary education should be that all children are given the opportunity to learn through a continuous and progressive programme of experience. Music is a way of thinking, a way of experiencing the world, a way of feeling and a way of interacting which is quite unique. Although it may share certain qualities, and characteristics with other disciplines or subject areas it exploits them in ways that are quite particular to music.

Rank these five options in the order of priority you would choose for teaching music.

I teach music:

- to promote the development of children's personal qualities (e.g. creativity, self-esteem, self-confidence)
- so that children can gain the mastery to express their personal thoughts and feelings.
- so that children will produce competent musical work and make informed musical judgments.
- so that children may become literate music 'consumers' — which means investing and taking pleasure in artistic experiences.
- as a way of supporting learning in other subjects, and/or as a basis for exploring personal, social and moral issues. [slightly adapted from Ross and Kamba, 1997]

Of course these statements are not mutually exclusive and you might convincingly argue that any one will enable the others to be pursued. It is a question of value and emphasis which will dictate where you put your energies, what teaching styles you adopt, what repertoire and activities you encourage, and what you encourage your colleagues to focus on in their teaching.

These statements might also be used to introduce discussion amongst the staff as a whole. If the word 'music' is replaced with 'arts' the debate can be broadened to encompass art, dance and drama in the school. It would be valuable to share views with other arts coordinators to discover how much common or distinct ground exists and to find ways of promoting the importance of the arts and developing opportunities for learning within the school.

Despite the need to embrace all aspects of the music curriculum in your role as coordinator, you are inevitably going to find that you are much more enthusiastic, skilled or confident about some things than others. People who have not had much in the way of a music education are often puzzled by the amount of specialism within music: being an accomplished performer on the piano does not mean that one knows anything about how to play the flute; playing fluently from notation does not mean that improvising or playing by ear comes easily; directing a choir is not the same as conducting an orchestra. These are clearly the results of interest and education and can be rectified to a certain extent, but it is unreasonable to expect one music teacher to provide the full range of skills and knowledge that might be considered desirable for a school. In Part 2 I will focus on these, and you might consider carrying out a review of your own specialist strengths in music to plan for professional INSET for yourself, or consider music expertise you might buy in, on occasion, or find amongst colleagues.

Such self-appraisal will contribute significantly to how you develop your role as coordinator. You cannot hope to advise and help others if you are unclear about your own capabilities.

Networking

Being the music specialist in a school can be quite isolating: there may be no other teacher with whom you can share your ideas or anxieties; you are so busy with extra-curricular activities that you miss out on the more general support and talk amongst colleagues. There may be few opportunities for you to meet with music teachers from other schools because you are all so busy, or there are limited resources for INSET available. Sharing experience and learning from peers is a vital part of professional development. There need to be regular occasions when your own theories and practice can be reflected upon, reaffirmed, challenged or developed.

On every occasion that I have been involved with INSET courses, as provider or participant, it is obvious that great value is given by teachers to the opportunity to meet other teachers; to learn from each other to strengthen morale and to attend to their own needs. With the reduction in LEA services there may be very little in the way of courses on offer. You may need to look nearer to home and contact music coordinators in neighbouring schools to set-up a 'self-help' group (this could be based on existing 'cluster' arrangements). You might also look further afield at regional or national music education associations which put on courses and conferences (see Part 5).

Chapter 2 Consultancy

I have referred to the role of consultant as distinct from that of coordinator. Coordinators do not automatically act as consultants whereas a subject consultant in school is probably the coordinator. Consultancy is seen by many music educators to be the most effective method of achieving curriculum development and change. During the early 1980s, Reading University School of Education pioneered a music consultancy course which was then emulated and developed by several other institutions and LEA advisory teams. Although many of the original courses have now ceased to exist the resonance of their work is strongly present in the work of many advisers, teacher educators and school-based teachers.

The approach originated in the development of advisory teachers' work in primary schools. It was recognised that very little long-term benefit was gained from one-off workshops or inservice courses. Real change only took place as a result of a sustained period of input and contact over time, from a specialist. The support would offer practical experience of music making for the teacher in a workshop or alongside children in class, demonstration lessons, supported practice, and advice on planning and management. The teacher's own subject knowledge and experience of music was recognised as the key to their confidence in teaching. If you look at the tone and content of books for primary music teaching from about the mid 70s, you will notice a clear shift towards the non-specialist audience: circle games, playground repertoire, sound exploration, graphic notation and using stories and poetry for composition become the main vehicles for musical learning. The emphasis is firmly on the ability of everyone to participate, learn skills and develop their musical imagination. These ideas did not come out of the blue but the target audience was new. It meant that a different language, free of specialist terminology, developed, and traditional musical skills such as using staff notation and playing the piano were downplayed. Music educators were keen to demystify music which was seen as a very elitist subject in education. In different ways Orff, Paynter and Murray-Shaffer pioneered and progressed this movement and their influence can still be keenly felt.

The belief that all of us are capable of participating, responding and expressing in or through music is now quite embedded in professional primary practice today. There did seem to come a point in the mid 80s where there was a feeling that music educators were almost suggesting that no specialist skills were really needed at primary level; I'm not sure that non-specialist teachers were very convinced by this. Now, I think, we have arrived at a more balanced approach. There is a recognition that trained music teachers are crucially important in primary schools for their specialist skills and knowledge in order to provide the depth of experience that children need, and to give clear and rigorous direction to the curriculum.

Another principle which contributes to this is that of the generalist class teacher. Primary music specialists, in my experience, want to have a class and teach the whole curriculum.

What is consultancy in music education?

Consultancy is a method of bringing about change in an individual or organisation. A person with expertise is asked to gather evidence and appraise the situation, individual or organisation with the purpose of helping to create change, improvement or development. The consultant aims to create a situation in which the consultee (or client) takes ultimate responsibility for what action is decided upon; this is done through discussion, negotiation, training input where appropriate and some mechanism for monitoring and evaluation. The ultimate goal should always be to achieve independence rather than dependence so that both parties can withdraw from the formal contract in the knowledge that the client is now better able to plan and teach with confidence, while the consultant reverts to the more general role of coordinator, able to offer advice and support when asked.

Aubrey (1989) identifies three types of situation which invite the attention of a consultant:

corrective	■	to solve problems of lack of achievement and poor quality performance,
progressive	■	to improve or develop the quality of provision in some way,
creative	■	to offer new directions or a fresh outlook.

In the context of this book the second situation is likely to be the most common and the one most appropriate for you as a colleague to undertake in your capacity as coordinator. The others are likely to need more objective and more specialised treatment such as that offered by a consultant from outside the school. Where they exist, this is an appropriate role for local education authority advisory staff, but there are also independent consultants who may be available.

The role of consultant is not to be taken on lightly and needs thought and probably some training. It is rare for a coordinator to be asked specifically to work in this way at interview. It is much more likely that you will gradually take on the role in the light of your assessment of what is needed to improve provision in your school. Your confidence and readiness to do this will also depend on your increasing experience and understanding both as a music teacher and as a professional colleague. Consultancy requires trust and respect on both sides and this takes time to develop. It is particularly difficult for a young, relatively inexperienced teacher to be accepted in this role by older colleagues even when you feel you have a lot to offer. I interviewed Clare when she was in her first term of her first appointment, after qualifying as a primary teacher with music as her specialism. She has gained the impression that most of her colleagues would be quite happy if she were to teach all the music in the school, however she does not want this to happen so is planning to gradually introduce a consultancy approach:

> ...when it actually comes to talking to other staff about the music in their classrooms I'm very aware that I'm new to the school and they are more experienced than me. I think that's going to be quite hard. I don't think I'm ready to do that yet, I need to leave it a few months and then I'll know them better as well.

Experienced coordinators I have talked with consistently mention the long time it takes to achieve the situation in which all teachers are, fairly confidently, teaching music to their own class. The time is, of course, lengthened by staff changes and one has to be quite altruistic in one's thinking about who will ultimately benefit from your work i.e. children in another school. Daphne started as a specialist and has gradually learned to see her role as including a consultancy approach. She has been in the same school for thirteen years and initially taught all the music. Now, all the teachers teach their own music with continuing support from her:

> When I first came here I was the specialist and I did all the KS2 music and virtually never saw my own class — only for Maths and English. Gradually as the thinking changed in Devon I began to see my role differently; so I first of all had to change the head's view, then he moved and when the new head came in it was actually easier to say 'this is how I want to work'.
>
> It was a big change for me — to stop thinking of myself as the sole specialist
>
> I wasn't entirely convinced by these new ideas to start with. I suppose, some of it was lack of confidence — it was the one thing I can do and you take that away from me because suddenly everybody else can do it as well. That was almost threatening; but then to see that I still have my specialism, because people still need the advice, the help... but I could see very much the role model and especially the male/female one. Boys who had a male teacher who was keen on football became keen on football, whatever your interest is so the children seem to sway towards that and if that teacher then taught no music it really was a downer on music. Whereas if the football teacher also taught music and enjoyed it, suddenly the children take to it. I had a classic example of that here with a male sports teacher who liked to listen to music himself but did nothing in his classroom. As a result of a consultancy course I was on I worked with him very closely on music and he started getting the children to compose and as they loved doing sport with him they also became really enthusiastic about music.

Julie is the music coordinator in a middle school (Years 4–7). She has taken eight years to get to the point where she feels confident that her colleagues are able to teach music consistently to their own classes. They have a positive attitude towards music: they use the resources she has provided and regularly consult her about their planning. The range and variety of musical activity has increased and she is able to devote her energies more to the really specialist aspects of the work such as extra-curricular performance groups and supporting the music teaching with the Year 7 classes. The eight years included a whole year without her own class so that she could devote all her time to consultancy; this had significant cost implications for the school but seems to have been money well spent. The impetus for this came from the findings of an inspection which was critical of the variation in provision between different years.

Philip is the headteacher of a primary school in Oxfordshire, he also acts as the music coordinator/consultant although there are other teachers with music expertise on the staff.

> What I want to do now is give people the opportunity to sit, observe and sometimes join in and then be able to take it on themselves next year. Then I would be on tap for them to invite me in to support their teaching, then in the third year they would feel confident enough to explore different ideas for themselves. I think of it in terms of at least a three year consultancy programme.
>
> As well as this, the schemes of work and resources are also being developed to support teachers in music; corridor conversations and inservice sessions. We have 2 INSET sessions planned for next term which I will co-run with one of the infant teachers who is a music specialist.
>
> Four out of twelve teachers are very confident with music and, for instance, the year 6 teachers do very good listening and appraising sessions but they wouldn't be so happy doing practical work with tuned instruments. But they're all capable of doing very good work in some aspects of music, it's just not broad enough. To avoid some classes having a rather limited experience teachers swap classes or join together in the main hall. I've done teacher appraisal on lessons and found that they are very well done.
>
> What we're looking at in Years 3 and 4 is to what extent we use a published scheme and how much we produce our own material.
>
> I would say that in any given week I'm involved in the music curriculum for about three hours a week, one way or another.

Yvonne coordinates music in a very large primary school in Leicester. Because there are twenty teachers the logistics of attempting to offer individual support over time to those who wanted or needed it were practically impossible. The solution here has worked very well. For a whole academic year the school bought in the services of an advisory teacher from the LEA. She worked regularly throughout the year taking demonstration lessons and providing ideas and support for individual teachers. This intensive input has quite rapidly improved the confidence and competence of all the teachers and allows Yvonne to now build on this in a more manageable way. She has produced a set of guidelines and schemes of work for every year, notes on progression, assessment and recording are included along with a list of resources (and where they are kept).

The music coordinator as consultant, is concerned with supporting the professional development of colleagues in order to improve the quality of music education for all children in the school. This might be done in a number of ways all of which involve the consultant working closely and sensitively with teachers. One of the features of this approach is that the consultant must be able to analyse and assess what is needed and what is appropriate for individual teachers. This is a refinement of the audit and review which will start as a means of looking at the child's experience of music education during its time in the school, identifying where the strengths and weaknesses are, and ultimately focusing on ways of capitalising on the former and reducing the latter. As has been described here and in many other publications, a main cause of patchy quality in curriculum music is class teachers' own perceived lack of teaching competence in music. I say 'perceived' because one of the main obstacles to music curriculum development is teachers' own narrow views of what music teaching skills are. This is an important aspect of the consultant's job: to re-educate colleagues about the nature of music as a curriculum subject, the ways children learn and the ways teachers might teach. The coordinator as consultant has certain advantages over an outsider when it comes to identifying problems and needs, and implementing improvements. S/he has detailed knowledge of the politics, procedures, resources, personalities and relationships: the culture of the school. This should lead to greater sensitivity, sympathy and insight. On the other hand, this familiarity might make it difficult to step back and view the situation dispassionately. Yvonne described her feeling that it is difficult being 'a prophet in your own land'. This is why, I believe, it is useful to think of the consultancy approach in a fairly formal way so that both you and your colleagues can maintain some professional 'distance' and confidentiality.

Although the consultancy process is a slow one there must be some recognition that it should take place within a finite period. An initial, fairly intensive period of a term should work well, followed by regular meetings (mutually agreed) and occasions when lessons can be observed to monitor progress and evaluate the teachers's achievements. A consultant cannot impose their own interpretation and solutions on colleagues. S/he must work in partnership to enable them to develop their own understandings and ways forward; this is not easy and draws on skills that we use in abundance with children but are probably less inclined to use with colleagues.

The skills of an effective consultant/coordinator are, in many ways, the skills of good teaching, with the added dimension of supporting and guiding two communities of learners: children and adult colleagues. In many schools where virtually all staff are responsible for a subject, teachers will shift between expert and generalist roles quite regularly during their professional work.

I have summarised those skills and qualities which seem most relevant to this context from those suggested by Kubr (1983) in Aubrey (1989):

The ability to
1   learn quickly
    observe and evaluate
    make good judgments
    think creatively and with imagination
    think on your feet

2   gain the trust and respect of colleagues
    relate easily and with sensitivity to others
    be tolerant
    to be a sympathetic and attentive listener

3   speak and write clearly
    explain and deconstruct concepts or processes
    motivate and encourage
    to give and receive positive and negative feedback in a
    tentative and non- judgemental way (Aubrey, 1991 p. 4)

4   act independently
take the lead or be lead
persevere
withstand pressures and cope with obstacles and
distractions
be good humoured and patient

5   admit mistakes and take advice
never betray a confidence

This looks a daunting list and does not include the central
requirement which is to have confidence in one's own subject
knowledge and teaching experience. This does not have to be
vast but needs to be secure enough that you can be flexible and
fluent in your advice and guidance to colleagues.

The consultant should work alongside the colleague in the
classroom so that theory and practice are being shared and
communicated in the real context. Time also needs to be set
aside for talking through plans and outcomes. The teaching
and learning take place through guided practice, discussion,
demonstration, providing ideas and resources, and building on
the teacher's strengths and interests.

The conditions necessary for successful consultancy

The support and understanding of the headteacher and the
school as a whole are of fundamental importance to the
success of this approach. It is the only approach which will,
in theory, lead to more music of a consistent quality and a
broader scope being taught by the existing staff in a school.
Greater continuity of experience, and therefore progress, in
learning for all the children in the school will be possible.
The headteacher needs to understand fully the concept of the
consultancy approach and initial discussions to share aims,
objectives and the resource implications are important. It
requires time and consequently money.

As consultant you will need:

- a mechanism through which you can gradually gain experience and knowledge of every age level in the school. You may only need to do this for ages with whom you have had little teaching contact. If you are a KS2 teacher you may want to spend time with reception and Year 1 children and vice versa with Year 6. This might mean arranging for teachers to swap classes or other cover being provided. Enlightened headteachers may see part of their role acting as an occasional supply teacher to enable teachers to observe each other or carry out consultancy work with colleagues.
- time to seek advice from other specialist sources such as LEA advisers, colleagues in other schools, attendance on a coordinator's course (such courses usually include references to or focus on consultancy techniques).
- staff-meeting and other INSET time (teacher days) in order to
  1 discuss with colleagues ways you might support them
  2 run practical workshops to introduce and develop teaching ideas
  3 lead discussion on curriculum development
  4 review and evaluate provision
  5 formulate policy
  6 introduce new resources (instruments or published teaching material)
  7 discuss assessment

(This is the most formal setting for your role as coordinator and consultant and it is important that you ask for and use the time you are offered.)

Daphne describes her use of meeting time:

> I've given each teacher a file which I've compiled. It sets out the policy and development plan; then for the Nursery right up to Year 6 I've taken the musical elements and then I've also written out the progression for playing, singing, performing.
>
> Alongside that they've also got what I expect them to cover during the year and then notes to accompany which get progressively more extensive as we go up the school. They will then plan their own lessons or units of work drawing ideas from these suggestions or devising their own. Every year group then gives me a copy of what they have planned on an A3 sheet; this happens every term for every subject with the same format. It includes what the focus is, possibilities for IT applications and what form the assessment will take.

> Also in this folder is a collection of practical games and activities for developing pulse, pitch and rhythm which I've picked up from all sorts of sources; a list of all the tapes and CDs in the school; all the instruments and some tips on how to play them; health and safety guidelines (taken from LEA publication).
>
> I knew that just giving it out might mean it would just go on a shelf so what I've then done is I've taken some 10 minute slots in staff meetings just to deal with one aspect; teachers are busy, they haven't got time to sit and read through all this so, for instance, I did a session on how to use a piece of music and look for the structure; one on vocal development...doing little bits now and then to keep focusing their attention on music.

The support and confidence of your headteacher will give a signal to the school community that music is valued. It recognises that, like a number of other subjects which involve practical skills and distinctive or rather specialised ways of thinking (science, design and technology, IT), teachers may suffer greater anxieties and misgivings about their abilities to teach them and consequently need more generous INSET provision. There is also a recognition of music's place in the curriculum as an area of experience important for all children not only those who show special interest or aptitude. It is all too easy for the management and parents to support the 'display' or performance elements of musical activity and to measure the quality of music learning in the school based on partial and selective evidence.

The consultancy process

As a result of some whole staff discussion or a practical ideas session you may find that an individual colleague approaches you for further help. This is the ideal first step as it is initiated by the 'client' rather than imposed. Also, through the process of auditing and reviewing music you should have identified colleagues who would benefit from your help.

The colleagues who are least resistant should be the ones you give your attention to, not the teacher you feel is in most need — the one who does nothing — but those who are keen to improve. You will not get very far with a reluctant or resentful subject.

When embarking on this approach for the first time it is a good move to work with someone you feel comfortable with.

As part of an inservice course for coordinators in Devon, course members were asked to choose a colleague to work with back in school and to plan to collaborate on a scheme of work which would result in the colleague gaining experience and confidence in teaching music to their own class. In recording the progress of the work we asked the coordinators to write a report based on some questions. The first was 'Who did you choose to work with and why?'

Their answers give evidence of their ability to identify what is likely to succeed:

> **Catherine**: choosing the teacher was easy since she'd expressed an interest in having some help already. She thinks she is 'totally unmusical' because she claims to be tone deaf. This is the result of a friend criticising her, some years ago, for singing flat. Despite my reassurance that she does sing in tune she doesn't believe me. She also teaches beginner recorders but does not see this as 'musical'.
>
> **Lucy**: I have chosen an NQT who started teaching at the school when I did. We team teach and have built up a close relationship. She wanted some help with music and I was keen to be observed and to get some feed back on my teaching.
>
> **Val**: I have chosen a teacher with whom I have a comfortable and mutually supportive relationship. She has given me much appreciated help in her role as history coordinator and was very willing to accept my advice with music.

What characterises Lucy and Val's choices is the reciprocal nature of the relationship they have, or seek with the chosen colleague. This seems to be an important factor when carrying out a consultancy with a peer. The chosen colleague will still have equal or superior status in other fields of professional work and this allows for maintenance of self-respect in an otherwise vulnerable situation.

The situation below is much more problematic.

> The teacher was really chosen by the head who was concerned about the music teaching in his class. He had previously worked in a middle school where he was not expected to teach music at all. As he had not sought help I had to tread carefully. My first breakthrough was at the end of the summer term when, as a whole staff, we worked on our year planning. He asked me for some suggestions for music, and although he rejected my detailed lesson plans he did take up one or two ideas. Subsequently he told me how much he was enjoying them. I support all the staff with written schemes of work but he is very resistant and I'm not sure how much effect I'm having.

All of these are examples of this initial 'contract' stage. In this case the impetus was the coordinator's attendance on a course and expectations being raised in the school that something should happen as a result.

There are other stepping-off points that may arise;
- the run-up or aftermath of an inspection (not ideal as this might produce a feeling of coercion)
- the purchase of significant new resources such as instruments or a published scheme
- a change of staff or responsibilities amongst the staff
- an opportunity for the school to become involved in a special music project with other schools or with professional musicians
- the appointment of an NQT or returner who is open to all offers of support.

Whether you intend to adopt a consultancy approach in your role in a significant way or not, you will still find yourself using some of the strategies and techniques associated with it.

In education as well as other professions and industry, it has been recognised that if one wants to change people's practice one has to change attitudes. People need to feel valued for what they do, and in control of it.

The actual consultancy programme can then get under way. Through listening to your colleagues you will learn about their perceptions of what they think they need, what they enjoy and what they feel anxious about. Agree on aims for your work together and decide on a programme of shared teaching sessions (perhaps every two weeks so that in the intervening week there is time for consolidation), observations and, ideally some non-contact time to discuss progress and plans. The aims might be very modest: feeling confident about using instruments, or learning how to lead listening activities, or incorporating composing into some rhythm work.

The headteacher will need to know what is to be attempted and how it will be evaluated, especially if extra resources are to be drawn upon. Again, formalising the process will give professional status and discipline to it. If this does not happen there is a likelihood that, for all sorts of reasons, things will fall apart. This happens very easily when everyone has a hundred other things to do and what you are asking feels risky or unfamiliar.

When you teach demonstration lessons, team teach or offer ideas, try to be sensitive to your colleague's preferred teaching style and avoid suggesting ways of working with which they will feel uncomfortable. Try, where appropriate, to draw on their subject strengths and work in a collaborative rather than a 'teach like me' mode. Be conscious of your use of specialist language and explain terms, perhaps provide a glossary.

Be realistic and pragmatic; work with no more than two colleagues at any one time and expect improvements to be gradual. There is bound to be a surge of enthusiasm to begin with, which will plateau as simple, initial games and activities give way to more demanding ones. You will find that helping teachers of younger children is easier because of the close match between the developmental stage and the teachers' elementary skills or inexperience. Teachers of Years 5 or 6 will be dealing with musical concepts and activities that are more sophisticated and therefore more demanding. Nevertheless, it should still be possible for generalist teachers to teach effectively and with understanding if they are supported by appropriate materials and advice. There is no curriculum area where teachers would expect always to know and understand more, and be more skilled, than all the children they teach.

The best possible outcome is that teachers will discover how much they and their children can enjoy music, and also that they will gain new knowledge and appreciation of their children's capabilities.

Monitoring and evaluation

Once the process is underway, and after the initial inputs, you will need to agree on a method of monitoring and assessing progress. Informal chats are useful but you will also need to have some written record to report back to the headteacher (see suggestion).

Suggestion

Use these headings
- Aims and objectives
- How we worked: timescale of process, classroom sessions, talk sessions, resources.
- Achievements (for teacher/s, for children)
- Problems
- What next?

The right colleague:

- a colleague who would welcome support of a general nature (NOT: returner; low morale)
- a colleague with whom you have a successful working relationship
- a colleague who has asked for ideas or advice in the past
- a colleague who has expressed interest but also nervousness about, for instance, using instruments
- a colleague who is musically active outside of school but does not know how to apply this in the classroom e.g. amateur singer; plays in a band etc.

The right vehicle:

- build on teacher's subject strengths
- build on to existing plans e.g. look for potential in topic work
- the teacher/s must feel they are in control of content and pace of the programme
- start with familiar territory: BBC broadcast, singing etc.
- use material you are confident with so that you can 'sell' it

Monitoring:

- notice classroom displays, sound tables . . .
- assembly presentations
- what you hear through walls
- use of resources
- formal or informal reviews and evaluations; chats in the staff room, planning sessions . . .

Raising the status of music:

- ask for staff development time
- involve whole staff in production of policy document even if you are ultimately responsible
- emphasise the importance of planning for progression and therefore the importance of assessment
- devise opportunities for 'publishing' (sharing) class music in assemblies, to another class, open days etc.
- educate parents and governors through presentations and practical 'workshops'
- improve and develop resources: have a list of needs so that whenever money is being bid for music is considered
- keep in touch with what is on offer in the region so that you can tap into professional music projects, LEA initiatives, etc. which offer curriculum enhancement for your children

MANAGING CHANGE

Although it is vital to have support from your headteacher — the quality of working relationships amongst the class teachers will determine the success of any development. There must be trust and respect. A balance needs to be struck between avoiding the feeling that music is either too difficult and arduous; or that it is merely fun and games (and therefore expendable).

Sustaining and developing confidence and practice:

- foster a professional approach to any work you plan and carry out with colleagues
- acknowledge and praise effort both formally and informally

The right time:

- a change of staff, especially positions of responsibility,
- new instruments purchased — sudden interest!
- OFSTED on the horizon
- OFSTED inspection identified room for improvement
- planned topic (by group of teachers or whole staff) offers opportunity for music focus
- a music or arts event planned in your locality (academic council; family of local schools, LEA initiative etc.) provides impetus for increasing involvement amongst colleagues
- GEST professional development course!

The right approach:

- prepare the ground by getting to know something about their teaching style, strengths and weaknesses
- This can be done through joint planning, shared teaching sessions, informal chat, classroom observation in a subject area they are very confident with
- share aims and objectives, don't be too ambitious
- agree a programme of support and try to stick to it

Subversion:

- offer music resources/ideas to support other subjects: art, creative writing, dance, humanities, technology . . .
- wean colleagues off their usual diet
- the children are your best advocates and lobbyists!

The brick wall:

- don't waste your energies on colleagues who are very negative or hostile
- concentrate on short-term achievable goals first
- remember that progress will be very slow when you are concerned with changing attitudes as well as practice

FIG 2.1
Managing change

35

Suggest that your client keeps a journal to record and reflect on their experiences of working with their class. As I have mentioned before, ask them to record examples of lessons and children's work in music. Try to make it possible for some collaborative work to take place, with both your classes.

At a stage when your colleague feels confident it would be valuable for you both to share the process and progress with the rest of the staff. You want to encourage your clients to become advocates for music!

This 'poster' (Figure 2.1) was produced by the members of an inservice course for coordinators in Devon. As a result of their own experiences of learning to use a consultancy approach in school they collected together their reflections, advice and warnings.

Part two

What music coordinators need to know

Music coordinators need to know about what is going on in their school, and how to maintain develop and improve it. They also need to know what characterizes effective teaching in music and how to identify and build on children's musical achievements. Knowledge about music itself is only valuable insofar as it enables you to be a confident music-maker, a sensitive and discriminating listener and an imaginative facilitator. Knowledge of different musical styles and traditions, and having an 'open' ear is of much greater value and relevance than possessing a Grade 8 certificate for performance; although a combination of all these would, of course, be very useful!

| Chapter 3 | Gathering information |

Before instigating change, development or new initiatives you need a comprehensive picture of provision throughout the school.

If you are new to the school as well, then clearly you will need a certain amount of time just to establish yourself with your own class and get to know how the school works. However, you will quickly find that you are picking up all kinds of impressions and information about what is or is not going on. At some point, perhaps towards the middle of your first academic year, you will need to start gathering evidence in a more systematic way. If you are already established in the school but have this new responsibility you should be able to start your research immediately.

You should design a format for this so that the information is coherently presented. Your school may have an agreed method of auditing curriculum provision but you may find that there are aspects of the music curriculum which are unique. Wheway and Paterson (1996) have produced a Music Policy disk which provides a very comprehensive and straightforward format by which the coordinator can not only record existing provision but also present plans for development. Many LEA curriculum support services have designed and published guidelines and checklists. Before designing your own format find out what is available, you may save yourself a great deal of time!

The following questions are for you, as coordinator, to address.

Policy and planning

Is there a written statement of policy for music?
When was it written and is it still relevant?

Are there written schemes of work for all classes in the school?
Who was involved in producing them (specialist, class teachers)?
Do they identify NC programmes of study?

Who teaches music?

Is music mainly taught through integrated topics or is it taught separately?
How is the music curriculum in the school reviewed and evaluated?

Music repertoire

What song books are used?
Is there a wide variety of listening material in good condition, and reflecting what teachers need? Do all teachers know and use it?
Does the repertoire used in lessons and elsewhere reflect a balanced 'diet' of music from a variety of traditions, styles and times?

Music learning

How long and how often are timetabled music lessons?
Is the time for music used flexibly?
How often are children exposed to and engaged with music, both in and out of the classroom?
Is there a balance between learning in and learning through music?

Do children learn in music through an integrated approach to listening, composing and performing or do teachers tend to focus on one at a time?

Are there opportunities for children to revisit repertoire or particular activities to experience at a more sophisticated level?
Is there clear evidence of progression through the school?

Are there opportunities for children to work in groups and individually?

Do children have opportunities to experience music combined with other art forms?

What provision is made for special needs in music (including those with exceptional aptitude)?
Are children encouraged and/or able to pursue their own musical interests?
Is extra-curricular activity planned to encompass and extend a variety of interests and abilities?
Do the musical activities offered in the school encompass the musical needs and interests of children's cultural backgrounds?

Music assessments

Do teachers generally have high expectations of children's abilities in music?
Are teachers expected to formally record their assessments?
Do teachers feel confident to assess learning in music?
Are assessments moderated in any way?

Teaching resources

Where does music teaching take place?
Is accommodation for music adequate?
Are the acoustic conditions for music lessons adequate (sound proofing, disturbance from other activities)?

Is there a reasonable selection of up-to-date published resources to support teachers' planning?
Are some aimed at true non-specialists (careful use of specialist language and minimal use of staff-notation; tapes)?
Do teachers use schools' broadcasts? Are they used selectively and integrated with school planning?
Is there a scheme (Silver Burdett, Lively Music, Nelson Music etc.) in place and is it well used?
Do all teachers have access to good quality audio equipment?
What IT resources are available, and do all teachers know and use them?

Are there enough classroom instruments for the needs of the school?
What condition are they in?
Where and how are they stored?
Are they accessible to all classes?

What human resources are available to the school e.g. visiting instrumental teachers, professional musicians and companies, animateurs (community musicians, dancers), parents and friends in the community?

Sharing music

On what occasions do children perform music to an audience other than their own class?
Are all children involved or does it tend to be the same minority?
How often do such performances include children's own compositions?

Answers to many of these questions will be easily come by. There can be still be a gap between what has been agreed on paper, what teachers say they do, and what is actually going on. Although time consuming, collating information about resources, timetabling, staffing, accommodation and the range of activity offered should not be contentious or sensitive. However, to evaluate the *quality* of what is going on will probably need a different approach.

The impressions you gain from the music you hear and observe will be the best indicator of this and one might assume that if there is a lot of sharing and presentations of music outside the classroom this is a good indication of activity inside the classroom. If there is not a tradition of this kind of performance activity you may need to go about your audit task in a more circumspect manner.

As a class teacher yourself it is often quite difficult to develop a good sense of what is happening in other classrooms. Unless the school has a policy of team teaching or is open plan, you may seldom be able to observe your colleagues. Many schools now expect teachers (especially where there are parallel classes) to plan together and through these planning sessions you will gradually glean information about the enthusiasms, expertise, and confidence of colleagues.

Think about a typical planning meeting.

- Is it always the same teachers (or only you) who raise the possibilities for including music in cross-curricular plans?
- Is the inclusion of music always dependent on your offer to work with other classes?
- Are the suggestions for music activity usually to do with finding songs which relate to the topic?
- Are the suggestions usually rather marginal or slight in relation to other subject inputs?

By attentive listening to your colleagues you will discover a lot about their attitudes and knowledge through what they do and do not contribute.

There are always likely to be colleagues with whom you do not work so closely and you need to find ways of learning about their strengths and weaknesses with regard to teaching music. There are many ways you can do this; some open and direct, others more subtle and careful (not necessarily devious!). You will need to consider which approach is the most diplomatic and which will achieve the picture that is most truthful.

If you are newly appointed to the role of coordinator you are in a strong position to ask direct questions of your colleagues. A change in personnel, roles and responsibilities, or management structure will help them accept the need for such research. It is important to ensure that everyone is clear about your purpose and what you intend to do with the information. An audit and review must be seen to be providing the information which will lead to improvements in the quality of music education taught throughout the school.

An initial information-gathering exercise could be a questionnaire for colleagues to complete. It needs to be concise, easy to complete and unambiguous in what you are asking. There are a number of ways to construct a questionnaire to get the information that you want. However, you must be aware that, as there is not much sense in making it anonymous, you need to make it as unthreatening as possible so that colleagues will answer fully and honestly without thinking that, if they admit to never singing with their class, they are going to find themselves on a compulsory singing course!

Decide what you want to find out and then what can be found out, most reliably, from a questionnaire. Find out if they have been used before and to what effect. This might involve talking your ideas through with the headteacher or another coordinator. Remember that respondents may answer in terms of what they think you want to hear rather than what is actually happening, so you cannot expect this exercise to give you an entirely accurate picture. You may want to find out about:

1   the variety of activity taking place
2   the quality of what is taking place
3   the repertoire used
4   what resources are used
5   the amount of time given to music
6   the frequency of activity
7   to what extent music is taught through other subjects
8   what individual teachers feel most and least confident about in teaching music

Points 1–8 could be difficult to achieve in a questionnaire format so consider dealing with these through observation or conversation.

In many of the other questions you are trying to find out what is happening across a range of possibilities so consider using a multiple choice format, for example:

Q. How often do the children in your class listen to music? (underline your answer)

A. Never   rarely   occasionally (once or twice a term)   once or twice a week   every day

Q. When the children in your class listen to music, is it (tick all that are relevant)

a) as background for other work e.g. art?
b) as accompaniment for dance or gymnastics?
c) as a stimulus for creative work in other subjects e.g. writing?
d) to support knowledge and understanding in another subject e.g. geography, RE?
e) as part of a music lesson?
f) for relaxation?

The point is that all of these answers are valid and appropriate but if, for instance, the respondent only ticks a) and f) and not e) then you will have gained some knowledge of how s/he sees this activity. Through listing a number of possibilities you may also have suggested ideas that the teacher may not have thought of. In a round about way you may have planted a new possibility in their mind. A questionnaire will also allow a respondent to write, confidentially, about particular concerns which might not come out in discussion. Always include space for other comments.

Questions should as much as possible be asking for positive rather than negative answers. Any line of enquiry should strengthen and affirm what teachers do already rather than undermine or focus on weaknesses. A questionnaire invites the respondent to complete the answers as a solitary activity with no opportunity for dialogue so it should be used in a fairly limited way and in conjunction with other methods.

Alternatively, you might ask for boxes to be ticked. Although less time-consuming than other kinds of questionnaire they tend to be rather reductionist with no room for commentary or explanation.

You will need to consider other methods when finding out about teachers' confidence in and attitudes towards music teaching. A method which is rather more friendly, is to carry out a self-assessment activity which is shared. In terms of raising awareness of the whole staff and integrating this initial research into the process of curriculum development, this is far more effective in terms of interest and involvement. There are several ways of conducting such an exercise, some more collective than others. I will suggest two which I have used with experienced teachers and student teachers. The process itself should offer the potential for participants to learn more about their own abilities as well as those of their colleagues, whilst developing their understanding of music education itself.

This exercise needs to be carried out in the context of a staff development session.

Suggestion

The Spider
The first two stages of this exercise are crucial so be prepared to give a good amount of time to them.

Stage 1: Ask the question: what skills, knowledge and understanding are necessary to teach music in primary school?

First ask each participant to jot down their own list of answers. When this has been done ask them to compare their own list with their neighbour's in the group.

Stage 2: Now explain to the group that their answers will be listed on a board (flip-chart) and as the list develops they may find that people have expressed the same points in different ways. The task of the group is to finally agree on the wording of each statement; and to try to limit the list to no more than 10 separate statements.

You might end up with something like this (taken from a student teacher group).

1 have enthusiasm for a wide variety of music
2 be able to read and write traditional notation
3 be able to sing simple songs with confidence
4 be a good listener
5 have a sense of rhythm
6 know how to organise practical music making for the whole class and groups
7 know the names of, and how to play, classroom instruments
8 know how to facilitate children's composing
9 know how to evaluate and assess progress and achievement in music
10 know how to plan for learning in music

You may disagree with some of these (for instance, I disagreed with 2 as a necessity: desirable but not essential); but it is very important that what you end up with is a result of the group's thinking not just yours. The discussion that takes place as the list evolves is enormously valuable in airing opinions and worries; and your role is to help them come to a consensus. You may want to contribute to their discussion but this must be done without undue influence. During this exercise you will learn much about your colleagues, not only about their feelings about music teaching but also about how they relate to each other.

Are they relaxed in each others' company?
Are there definite cliques?
Do certain people dominate?
Are they taking the activity seriously or being flippant (often a defence mechanism!)?
Are they able to admit to problems with music?

Hopefully you will learn something about how they might respond to your role as a coordinator with the job of changing and developing their practice.

Stage 3: This activity is, again, individual. Each person has a sheet of A4 plain paper on which they draw an oval or oblong in the centre. It should be big enough to accommodate their first name. They then consider each statement and draw a line from the edge of the box towards the outer reaches of the page. The more confident, or able they consider themselves to be the longer the line. Each line is numbered accordingly. Each person should end up with a kind of profile, like a ten-legged spider, which should provide a fairly clear picture of perceived abilities amongst the whole staff. The results of this exercise can then lead to some discussion about what kind of individual or whole staff development work is needed.

[This same exercise might be used to look at the music curriculum as a whole, in relation to what is happening in school, so that you can prioritise areas for attention. Children could also assess their own music learning or evaluate a composition project using this approach.]

Structured discussion

At some point you will need to generate some discussion about values, principles and ideals. You will need to make a decision as to whether to do this early on in the process i.e.

as part of the audit/review stage; or introduce it after a period of staff development, at which point it might act as a useful mechanism for reviewing the school's policy document for music.

Again this activity could be used in all sorts of contexts — it proves to be particularly useful when tackling issues related to personal views as it offers a certain degree of objectivity for the whole group.

In a staff meeting to discuss the development of the music curriculum there needs to be a way of structuring and encouraging debate amongst the staff. Although you may have well developed views and ambitions of your own it is vital that you progress together, as a whole staff, otherwise colleagues may feel coerced and resentful. It may seem easier to present your policy and use the meeting to talk it through but this will not necessarily lead to colleagues feeling involved or responsible for its implementation.

Draw up a series of statements with which respondents can agree or disagree. You could purposely include some fairly outrageous statements which will provide some light relief and also lead to unified responses, for example:

- All children should be given the opportunity to learn a musical instrument.
- Children who show particular aptitude for music should be offered extra musical opportunities.
- We should have a concert or show with music at least twice a year.
- Children who cannot sing in tune should be discouraged from singing.
- Children learn best when they have a designated music lesson once a week.
- Children sing better when accompanied by the piano.
- At KS1 children should engage in some music activity every day.
- Children should be introduced to staff notation in Year 2.
- Only 'classical' music should be listened to in school.
- Contemporary music, apart from pop music, is too difficult for young children to understand or appreciate.
    . . . and so on.

The statements can focus on any issue you want to raise and could include re-worded statements you have heard made by colleagues or teachers elsewhere.

Write each statement on a plain postcard, shuffle them and place them on the table or floor around which the staff are seated. Each teacher, in turn, picks up the card on the top, reads it out to the group and immediately responds to it. Some general discussion then takes place and the statement is either accepted, refined, revised or rejected and an alternative adopted.

The discussion may need chairing, depending on the numbers involved, and someone to scribe. If you take on these roles it removes you from being heavily involved in the discussion, which could be useful as colleagues might be otherwise too ready to defer to you as the specialist. As a result of your research you should be able to make some sense of the abilities and attitudes of your colleagues.

Suggestion

Consider each member of staff in terms of their ability to facilitate or obstruct curriculum development. Plot each member of staff along a line: the far right is your ideal practitioner the far left is the teacher who does no music at all and actively resists involvement.

	A	B	C	✡

e.g. Mr A. has never taught any music and is quite happy to swap with a colleague so that he teaches their PE while his class have music...most resistant.

Mrs B. uses BBC broadcast material and sometimes further develops a suggested activity with her class. Is interested but unsure of what else she could do...towards the middle.

Miss C. has tried some circle games, and instrument exploration, teaches dance and often incorporates listening to music into topic work, not confident about teaching songs...least resistant.

This kind of exercise should help you decide on which teachers are teaching music most effectively, which are open to staff development, and which would probably not easily respond to your offers of help. When other evidence has been gathered you will then be able to draw up a detailed profile of what is happening and this can help in planning short, medium and long-term aims for curriculum development. It is clearly sensible to work with those colleagues who are most willing as this will have a more immediate and lasting impact on music provision.

An exercise such as this could be used to look at all manner of factors which contribute to the provision and quality of music learning: you could include accommodation, timetabling, and resources all of which can work for or against your aims.

Further evidence

Apart from focusing on what teachers tell you about what they do, or what they reveal about their opinions and attitudes, you will need to evaluate the quality of children's learning in music: singing, instrumental work, responses to music, ability to listen, dance, and compose. Assemblies in which different classes plan and present a topic can reveal a lot about what teachers feel confident about and what they value. The quality of singing at assemblies or singing practice; children's ability to sustain attention and interest when listening to music; their reactions to using instruments in a music session; their readiness to participate in music making are all indicators of positive and rewarding experiences.

For on-going evidence (not just to do with an initial audit) you should consider the following methods which I have collected from teachers:

- issue each class teacher with a blank audio tape and ask them to record examples of children's compositions, class singing, group work which arise from class lessons. This will be valuable on a number of counts:
  1 as a record of practical work to help in assessment
  2 as a record of work which the children are proud of
  3 as a means for the coordinator to monitor the quantity and quality of activity.
- suggest that children keep a music diary to keep their own record of achievements in music, activities they particularly enjoyed, music they enjoyed listening to, events etc.
- this idea might be incorporated into a method of appraisal through which the child and the teacher comment on achievements in music learning.

■ gather together a group of children from a particular year (chosen to represent differing abilities in music) and invite them to talk about the music they have been doing in class. What they have enjoyed, found difficult, what new skills they feel they have acquired. This last idea came from Rob:

> Well, this last term since September I've monitored Years 2 and 5. I sit in on planning sessions and conferencing children. This involves a session where I have three children from each class so there are 9 altogether for a year group and we sit down with a tape recorder. I have three or four questions on aspects of the music work they've been doing; like 'what songs have you learned?, could you sing that to me?
>
> Why would people sing a song like that?' (this was from a history related topic on the 1930s and 40s).
>
> 'Have you done any composition, can you talk to me about it, how did you put it together?' Open questions as much as possible to allow them to talk. This strategy is used with Art as well, there's also review sheets for children to write about how they feel about their own work in art or music.
>
> I'm attempting to evaluate the work which is going on in the classroom through the children's eyes so I chose a high, middle and low ability child from each class. Partly because of OFSTED. I've only done this once but it's going to become a regular thing. It was really useful and so enjoyable to sit down and talk with these children. The majority of the children talked quite freely and that tells me that a lot must have been going on.

As you go about this audit you will soon discover that a large part of your attention is on what other teachers are doing: how they feel about teaching music, what they teach and what they value in music learning. Without knowledge of these it will be very difficult to build on, or change practice and provision.

Chapter 4   Subject knowledge for effective teaching

Many teachers who are responsible for music in their school are often quick to tell me that they are 'not really a specialist', and I am not always sure what they mean by this. It usually transpires that they have not studied music at higher education level or did not train as a music teacher. Having a degree in music does not lead automatically to the kinds of musical skills and knowledge which are appropriate for teaching; in fact it can sometimes be something of an obstacle. Degree level study is highly specialised and often very narrowly focused; not all music degree courses develop practical music-making skills and graduates who come into training for primary music may have had little or no opportunity to improvise, play by ear, sing, dance or explore a wide range of musical styles and traditions. Primary teachers of music need to be able to do all these.

The other criteria which define the 'specialist' are playing the piano competently, reading notation, and having knowledge of classical music. Again, I would consider these to be useful but not necessarily essential.

What is much more important is that whatever the musical experience, enthusiasm and knowledge the teacher posesses, they are able to translate it into appropriate activities for their children and use it to inform their understanding of what constitutes learning in music.

In this chapter I have attempted to draw together aspects of subject knowledge and knowledge about teaching and learning which should be well established in the practice of an effective coordinator. This is not a manual on how to teach music nor a regurgitation of official curriculum documents. My focus of attention is on those aspects of practice which will be central to the concerns of your colleagues.

There are basic requirements, desirable requirements and skills or enthusiasms which can add a particular character to the musical life of a school. Basic requirements are those which all music coordinators must have or need to acquire if they are going to be effective.

Enthusiasm for music as a practical activity

You are the model not only for the children you teach but also for your colleagues. Your enthusiasms will 'rub off' on those who work with you. You cannot be enthusiastic about everything musical, and teachers invariably have their favourite musical styles (folk, jazz, baroque) and medium (singing, steel band, recorders etc.). What has to be remembered is that your responsibility is to providing a well balanced curriculum for all children — and this needs to take account of the need for breadth. There may well be a feeling of conflict here; between providing a very rigorous and high quality education based on, say, your specialist interest in English folk music, and offering a range of repertoire some of which might be less familiar or less attractive to you. The danger is that you may feel you do such repertoire a disservice by presenting it in a less convincing way.

A sensible way to proceed is to accept that we will all teach to our strengths and passions (this may be what attracted us to teaching in the first place) but recognise where you might have to draw on the expertise of others to provide the required breadth. This can be achieved in a number of ways:

■ through the audit you will, perhaps, have discovered colleagues who have musical interests or abilities different from yours. These should be encouraged and supported so that children gain from such diversity as they progress through the school;

- make links with the local secondary school and/or FE college — many institutions now have IT and recording equipment which might be accessible during certain periods. Encourage GCSE or 'A' level music students to visit your school to perform, help in class music lessons, teach small groups recorder/guitar etc., make recordings of children's performances of their own compositions. Act as performers for children to compose for etc.;
- find out about professional musicians or companies offering workshops, projects or residencies to schools;
- find out through your regional arts association about community musicians/animateurs and performing groups;
- consider developing your own skills and knowledge through courses, summer schools or joining a local group. Through your own music making outside school you may find valuable expertise amongst amateur or semi-professional musicians;
- contact your LEA advisory support services, if they exist, who should have information about other music teachers in your area;
- through in-service courses you can make useful contacts.

As money has become tighter and workloads have increased this 'nourishment' for teachers has become more scarce. When teachers find the means to attend a workshop or course, the reward and spin-off can go far beyond expectations. Refreshment to one's own practice can be enough in itself. Teachers quickly forget how enjoyable it can be to be a learner; to work through practical music-making activities with others; to learn and sing new repertoire; to take part in a drumming workshop. It is easy to forget the particular value of music for *us* as a social, physical, expressive and therapeutic experience which we need as much as our children do.

Singing

Suggestion

Try to answer these questions based on your own experience and observations. Are there some questions you find difficult to answer? How can you find out more?

In what circumstances, and for what purposes do children sing in school?
Do all teachers sing with their own class?
Do children have the opportunity to sing unaccompanied?
Do children have the opportunity to sing on their own or in a small group?
What is the usual means of accompaniment?
Does the song repertoire reflect a range of music from different times and places?
Does the song repertoire reflect the need for increasing vocal and musical demands as children develop?
Do children use their voices when improvising or composing?
Do boys participate in singing with enthusiasm?
Are there any strategies for helping children who sing out of tune?
Do children generally enjoy singing?
Is the singing in the school of good quality?

Answers to these questions will help you decide what needs attention in terms of guidance for colleagues, resources and your own knowledge of singing. The quality of singing in the school will undoubtedly be a reflection of how positive an image it has as an activity for staff and children. It does suffer from being seen as an unquestioned part of primary school culture, a good thing in itself and not subject to the same scrutiny as other activities might attract. One does not want to destroy its social role but there must be attention given to the quality of experience and the potential for learning that singing can offer.

The value of singing

Singing is the most fundamental means of musical expression we have. We sing for many reasons and in a variety of contexts:
- to develop language and speech through new vocabulary, rhyme and articulating words
- to develop a feeling for the rhythm in words
- to join with others in collective worship or celebration
- to communicate our feelings to others (love song)
- to comfort (lullabies), to rouse, to tell a story (ballads)
- to participate in a social activity: to promote a sense of community and well-being
- to accompany ourselves (children often improvise songs while they play)
- to consolidate or support learning in other subjects: number, history, PE, geography

In terms of learning in music, singing:
- has the potential to be the most expressive medium for our music making

- is the most effective way to develop a sense of pitch and to develop a good 'ear'
- with movement, develops the ability to keep time, internalise a pulse and perform rhythmically
- provides accessible and appropriate means through which children can understand musical elements, texture and structures
- provides ways of getting to know the cultural and social value of music through songs for different people and occasions

Repertoire

Just as coordinators of other subjects will recommend particular ideas, or resources to colleagues, you will need to be constantly adding to your list of songs which you can teach or offer to colleagues.

You should aim for songs which are appropriate to different stages in vocal development, varied in style and mood, musically interesting and satisfying.

Song repertoire does not have to be relentlessly cheerful and rhythmic. There is a danger that we neglect the songs which evoke feelings of sadness or where the words tell a melancholy story. Music provides a powerful means of expressing feelings we cannot or do not want to communicate in other ways.

Some songs can be learned quickly (repetitive, vocally straightforward) They will serve as a warm up or to reinforce a particular vocal or musical skill. Songs which are of value for their immediacy and accessibility should be for everyday singing in the classroom, and the playground. These songs are 'caught' rather than taught.

At the other end of the spectrum are songs which are musically more complex, more expressive, communicating more developed musical ideas and lyrics. Such songs will demand some attention to interpretation, more vocal control and accuracy.

A great deal of the song material available to schools is trite both musically and literally. Much of it borrows from pop

Suggestion

The singing repertoire should include:
Call and response songs
Echo songs
Action songs
Rounds
Story songs
Partner songs (where two independent songs harmonise when sung simultaneously)
Simple part-songs
Songs to accompany simple dances
Raps
Songs in different languages
Songs from different traditions
Songs from different times
Pentatonic songs
Blues

music styles which do not always sit very comfortably on children's voices. Pop songs are usually for one or two singers who use their individual vocal style to colour the vocal line. When a whole class sing this flexibility is lost and the character of the song may change.

We often choose a song for wholly non-musical reasons — because it fits the topic or the event. It may be that there is an alternative song which will fit the context just as well and is more musically interesting or appropriate. Your role as coordinator requires you to promote musical experiences of good quality for the children in your school and singing forms a substantial part of that experience.

Suggestion

Review your own song repertoire to see how comprehensive it is. Consider categorising song material in a variety of ways so that it can be used by teachers for different music learning and draw their attention to the potential for developing transferable skills;

For instance:

KS1 'We're Sailing Down The River'
develops:
- social interaction (making a circle, choosing partners, dancing together)
- rhythmic movement
- musical repetition
- legato singing with a fairly slow pulse and a rocking rhythm ($^6_8$) contrasted with a bouncy faster second action which needs clear articulation
- number work.

KS2 'Calypso' by Jan Holdstock (from Flying A Round)
Provides experience of:
- rhythmic articulation and syncopation
- octave pitch range
- 3-part round requires confident independence in both rhythmic and melodic singing, possibility of instrumental or vocal ostinati parts for individuals or small groups, introduces rhythm patterns typical of calypso style.

Some published schemes have produced this kind of analysis as a table and although I am not suggesting doggedly going through every song you use in this way, it is a useful exercise to do not only for yourself but with colleagues. In an INSET session on singing, for instance, you could present a number of songs that are familiar and ask them to look closely at them in this way. This should help them to become more aware of the teaching points in a particular song and also act as a way of increasing their own subject knowledge.

You will need to remind your colleagues and instil in your children the recognition that singing is a physical activity which involves the whole body. When singing is thought of in this way it will lead to more appropriate approaches: to accommodation, context, preparation and timing.

Accommodation

Children need enough room to stand comfortably — upright but relaxed, feet a little apart and arms at each side. Sitting cross-legged on the floor is the worst possible position as the torso is crushed and breathing restricted. You can sing anywhere but some spaces are more rewarding that others. A room with a fairly high ceiling, a partially carpeted floor and some curtaining should provide a pleasantly resonant acoustic. Rooms which are full of books, shelving, carpeted, acoustic tiles on the ceiling and fabric covered display boards will soak up sound and provide a very 'dry' acoustic which does not allow the singing sound to resonate in the space. It makes singing hard work and less rewarding.

Many schools will have spaces which approximate to these descriptions — the hall being the former, classrooms being the latter. Unfortunately, even where there is a designated music room it may have been decorated to insulate rather than resonate the sounds in the room. The hall, on the other hand, may be over-resonant but this is easier to deal with by the addition of fabric (curtains, display boards).

Clearly it is not possible to have a purpose built singing space but it is important to recognise the significance of the space we sing in, in terms of motivation and musical reward. It is also useful to consider how a space might be improved acoustically through redecoration or minor alterations. You will also need to be aware of the effect of moving from one space to another. The children have learned and rehearsed their songs in one space and go to the church or a secondary school hall for the performance, suddenly their sound is lost in the much bigger or loftier space. It can be quite unnerving. Try to ensure some rehearsal or warming- up time in the performance space.

Timing

As with so much early musical development, singing for 5–10 minutes every day is preferable to half an hour once a week. This is particularly true at KS1 but will be beneficial with all ages. Singing well should be physically invigorating and quite tiring. Where singing is part of a timetabled music lesson it should be subject to the same attention to learning aims as any other activity and form an integral part of the lesson along with composing and listening.

Singing for all

For some colleagues singing may be the aspect of the music curriculum they are most comfortable with. Many are happy to sing with children but not with their peers. For others it is a no-go area. If you have someone in this latter category you probably need to suggest activities that avoid singing, at first. The important thing is to try to instil confidence in your colleagues through providing appropriate resources, encouragement and guided practice. There are no real shortcuts to developing confidence but it is important to persuade your colleagues that a) they can all sing, and b) they can all, with practise, improve their singing. Teachers do not have to be wonderful singers to sing with their children. If we consider singing to be an ordinary activity for children, so it must be for their teachers.

A lot of activities which are close to singing can be suggested:
- choral speaking,
- playing with vocal sounds — sound effects, circle games for listening, sequencing, improvising with vocal sounds rather than instruments. (Listen to *Stripsody* by Cathy Beberian, Sheila Chandra's *Zen Kiss*, scat singing in jazz),
- using spoken language as composing material (see 'When Words Sing', Murray Schafer (1972) and 'Alligator Raggedy-Mouth', Hanke and Leedham (1996)),
- rapping,
- reciting poetry.

All of these will offer a path towards singing for the teacher but also provide creative and technically appropriate activities in their own right.

There are now many song collections, and teaching materials which include songs recorded on tape or CD. These vary in quality and are not always suitable to be played as the model for your children. Make a point of listening to the tape before offering it to colleagues. The good examples use voices which are natural and unforced i.e. like a teacher singing. Probably the best tapes are those which use children and include accompaniments separately so that the song can be learned unaccompanied.

You will need to advise colleagues on the pitfalls which may be created by using pre-recorded material to learn songs. To a lesser extent this can also include schools' broadcasts. The difficulty being that the performance on tape is a finished performance, up to speed and well polished. The process of teaching a song will invariably require the need for stopping and starting, repeating passages, providing visual cues through hand gestures ('landscaping') and responding to what is heard to improve and refine the performance. Probably the ideal use of a taped performance is as a means by which the teacher learns the song prior to teaching it, as a model of a good performance and to provide an accompaniment once the song is learnt.

Another potential source of confident singing models to help unconfident teachers is other children — older children in the school who can be invited to help with teaching songs to younger children. This already happens in many schools with reading and would be of general benefit to all concerned. Older children could also provide accompaniment (live or recorded) and this might offer opportunities for children who are learning instruments to have experience of arranging and performing.

A staff choir or regular singing workshops are the most direct ways in which singing confidence can be addressed. Apart from the professional development this will provide, it might

Suggestion

Tape record two or three sessions in which you are teaching songs and afterwards see if you are able to note the stages of the teaching process and the skills you are using.

also be a great source of pleasure and relaxation to the staff. A school in Somerset involves the staff choir in performance events such as Christmas concerts, and has made a real difference to attitudes to singing amongst staff and children. If singing is for all, *all* must be seen and heard singing.

Teaching a song

There are basic steps in this process which should be adhered to regardless of the complexity of the song and the experience of the teacher. As a confident teacher of music you might find it difficult to analyse what you do when you teach a song (rather like an experienced driver attempting to deconstruct the skill of driving for a learner).

Here is a list of points which should contribute to successful learning and a musical performance:
- know the song inside out (at least the first verse and chorus off by heart) so that you can sing it to the children fluently and convincingly;
- avoid teaching from the piano, guitar is more sympathetic and less dominant but unaccompanied is best;
- teach songs by ear rather than from word sheets or song books. If there are lots of verses you might write them up after the first verse and chorus are learned. Introduce notated songs when you feel it is relevant to chidren's learning and it will support their understanding;
- recognise that the way you perform it will communicate to the children — conviction, expression and clarity are all important;
- make eye contact and stand/sit with good posture;
- ask the children to listen for repeated rhythms or phrases. Discuss the words and character of the music;
- young children (R/Y1) will invariably join in straight away, regardless of whether they know the song. This is fine, although you will need to gradually encourage listening then singing (use a hand signal to reinforce this turn-taking);
- songs with lots of repetition built in are helpful because in the course of the performance the children will be exposed to the tune and words enough times to have learned it there and then. One might describe this as the song being 'caught' rather than taught;

- teach simple songs as a whole; if you use the line-by-line approach try to make this continuous i.e. avoid giving instructions and pausing during the process;
- use hand gestures ('landscaping' the melody line) to lead the singing;
- as the song is learned through repetition vary this so that it does not become tedious; sing very quietly, sadly, on one breath, angrily. Divide the class in half and ask each half to take turns to sing the song; or alternate line by line;
- discuss speed, dynamics and where to breathe;
- agree on how to begin (the starting note needs to be sung or played);
- add accompaniment when song is secure;
- teach a new song over two or three sessions, do not spend a large amount of time at one sitting.

Encourage children to sing solos or with just a few others. This can be done within a song: call and response or echo songs, particular verses, or as a complete performance. Children might like to record themselves singing a song they particularly like or have invented themselves. These will provide the teacher with useful assessment opportunities and also help children hear themselves. In most school singing activity children are singing as a class or in larger groups. This will not help children hear themselves and improve their tuning or tone quality. Solo or small group singing may be all that is needed to help certain children develop their intonation. For others who find themselves 'growling' below everyone else, more guidance will be needed.

Improving singing

❝ *Research into the singing behaviour of young children has shown that any class is likely to contain children who, between them, exhibit a wide range of accomplishment. . . . This range might well extend from a child being able consistently to sing with a high level of vocal accuracy to a vocal behaviour where it is unclear whether the child is speaking or singing. However, reasearch evidence is clear that every child has the potential, and is likely to be able, to sing in tune with appropriate teaching strategies and support.*
(Durrant and Welch, 1995)

Teachers first need to know that children develop their ability to sing in tune at different ages. There may be several reasons for this:

■ the normal development of the voice varies from one child to the next;

■ the pitch range which can be used comfortably may be quite limited in 4 and 5-year-olds;

■ lack of experience at home and school: children who have never been sung to and encouraged to sing until they start school are likely to have very underdeveloped singing voices in pitch range, tuning and strength;

■ children with some hearing impairment;

■ children who have suffered with intermittent hearing loss due to infections causing 'glue ear', children whose natural singing pitch is lower than average.

Remind teachers that 'nobody ever learnt to sing in tune by not singing at all' (Mills, 1991). Encouragement, inclusion and practise will always improve things.

Use circle games for:

■ exploring the voice

■ improvising

■ pitch-matching

■ breathing exercises

■ rhythmic articulation

With younger children include songs and singing as part of everyday routines such as singing the register, tidying up, end of the day etc.

When choosing and recommending songs look at the pitch range and how the melody line moves: diatonic steps and small intervals are easier than chromatic (semitone) movement and big leaps. Where songs are unaccompanied it is easy to start on a lower or higher note to make it suit the children. Match songs to voices rather than ask the voices to struggle to match the demands of the song. Encourage quiet singing, if children are continually told to 'sing up' they will end up shouting rather than singing. Vocal strength comes from breathe control and small children will develop this slowly as they grow in size.

Research has shown that boys do seem to have more difficulty with intonation than girls (Bentley, 1968). If this is a result of vocal development lagging behind girls or lower natural pitch range, then the strategies suggested above should help. However, it may well be just as much a problem caused by social and cultural conditions:

- there are very few male teachers in schools to provide positive role models for singing
- media images of male singers tend to be solo pop or rock singers who may have adopted a rather idiosyncratic vocal style which does not fit the kind of singing teachers encourage
- adult male singing in a group may be associated with football chants which tend to be sung in what I call an 'anti-singing' style (raucous, chest voice)
- as with stereo-typing of certain instruments, choral singing may suffer from being seen as something girls do
- the words of songs may not appeal to boys

Male role models and choice of repertoire should help to overcome some of these perceptions, but it is important to remember that singing is only one means of making music and some children will be more enthusiastic about other activities.

Assembly and whole school singing practice

One of the most typical responsibilities of the music coordinator is leading hymn or singing practice. In 1994 I carried out a small research project to find out how music specialists (mostly in the early stages of their careers) managed it in their schools and what they felt about it.

I discovered that in 36 primary schools across the country every one had some kind of singing session for the whole school or at least for each Key Stage, and all but six respondents were responsible for leading it.

> *Amongst these . . . most had inherited the tradition. Seventeen of these teachers expressed quite strongly negative feelings about what happened in their school. They doubted whether it contributed much to the planned music curriculum in singing experience or repertoire . . . 'I don't think the children get much*

out of it' and 'other teachers see it as non-contact time' were typical comments. In general, larger schools had one session each for younger and older children but there were exceptions to this: a primary school with 18 teachers expected the music teacher to take the whole school. In her response she expresses real concern about this: 'I don't agree with whole school singing practice. It is sometimes quite upsetting for the children who cannot read the words and the youngest get very little out of it'.
(Hennessy, 1996)

Almost all those who felt negatively about singing practice in their school had no support from other teachers and where a teacher was present they were only there for discipline purposes. On the other hand, responses from the other 50 per cent of respondents were much more heartening:

❛ *many of the teachers who felt positive had made concerted efforts to make the sessions fun, and focused on a variety of activities: rounds, action songs, rhythm games and some use of instruments. In a small school a singing session for all the children worked well, with older children providing good models and vocal support In a large school it seemed better practice to divide sessions into narrower age bands e.g. Y3–4, and Y5–6. Several teachers in the survey suggested that it had great value as a social activity; and a teacher in a school where a large percentage of the children spoke English as their second language felt strongly that it provided good opportunities for developing language through singing. This teacher had established some imaginative strategies: choir members teaching/leading the songs, and sharing songs in other languages lead by E2L children (including Somali, French and Arabic).*

*It seems that the most significant factor in all this is the involvement of other teachers. For good management and promoting singing as an activity for **everyone** it is vital that the school as a whole take an interest and support the specialist.*

If this kind of session is being included as part of curriculum time for music you, as coordinator, must look hard at how it supports music learning for all children, and how it connects with other music work in the school. You may well have to make yourself unpopular if you do not want to continue a tradition which allows most of the staff some non-contact time but is of doubtful educational value to everyone else!

If it is to continue insist that
- separate sessions are scheduled (perhaps less frequently) for infants, lower and upper juniors; or at least KS1 and KS2
- other teachers are actively involved in the sessions
- sessions are short (no more than 30 minutes, less for the youngest children)
- where possible, new songs are taught within class-sized groups

Instrumental work

This section is concerned with what is generally called 'classroom percussion' rather than instruments which are taught by specialist teachers and in elective groups (see Chapter 9).

In some schools you may still find instruments which reflect the trends of the past forty years: triangles, tambourines, coloured rhythm sticks, small cymbals and sleigh bells from the era of the percussion band; tuned percussion including chime bars, recorders and tambours reflecting the appearance of Orff instruments in the 60s and an ever-expanding range of instruments from all over the world which mark the interest in music of other cultures which took off during the 80s.

Using instruments in music lessons worries many generalist teachers. Their own lack of knowledge of what instruments are called and how they should be played, and their nervousness about managing whole class activities create obstacles to confident practice. Children tend to become excited when given instruments to play and whilst this is inevitable it is also compounded if the instruments are rarely used. Lack of familiarity and experience lead to exuberant and uncontrolled responses.

The most effective way to overcome the teachers' own anxieties and lack of experience is to provide some practical workshops for the staff. These will allow them to explore and experiment with instruments and learn some basic playing techniques. You will also be able to model ways of organising instrumental work in the classroom and explain the practical issues that arise.

It is very important that good habits of handling instruments and general behaviour are established. Teachers learn to do this in PE and other practical subjects and need to adopt certain routines for music also. These will depend very much on where the lessons take place which, in turn might affect how teachers include instrumental work in their plans.

If the school has a designated room for music the instruments should be readily available. If music happens in a variety of places (classrooms, the hall, studio) then the teacher will need to assemble the instruments beforehand: it should be perfectly possible for all but the smallest children to carry small crates or trays of instruments. You might suggest that each class appoint three or four instrument 'monitors' who are responsible for this and making sure instruments are cared for. Larger instruments such as a bass xylophone or a keyboard should only be moved by teachers (See Chapter 15).

When approaching practical music making for the first time it is a good idea to avoid using instruments altogether. This will allow the inexperienced teacher to focus on the development of fundamental musical behaviour through listening, performing and composing; and allow the children to focus on the more controllable sound sources i.e. voices and body percussion (clapping, clicking, stamping etc). Music starts with these both developmentally and historically: the most expressive and immediate musical instrument is the human voice. Body movements are not only an instinctive response to music but also instigate music making. Activities which develop many of the coordination skills, aural sensitivity, responses to visual cues and symbols, and the musical understanding necessary to play an instrument can all be established without instruments (see Suggestion).

All of these foster the general skills necessary for playing any instrument and, although I am not advocating an instrument-free music curriculum, it is important to give time to establishing teachers' understanding and confidence.

Suggestion

Consider this list of activities and write down three activities for each one which only need the voice, or body sounds.
- controlling dynamics (including silence)
- controlling speed
- exploring timbre
- maintaining a steady pulse
- rhythmic articulation and fluency
- imitating melodies
- reading and interpreting notations
- improvising and composing
- performing independently of others within a piece

The other side of this argument is that instruments are an important musical resource which should be exploited fully in the context of primary music-making. They provide a great range of sounds which are distinctly different from vocal sounds in terms of timbre, dynamics, pitch and articulation. Children should have the opportunity to expand their experience and knowledge of the world of sound. Percussion in particular connects children with the physical nature of music; through the energy and character of physical gesture musical expression is made and communicated.

Many children will be more attracted to music if given an instrument to play. It seems at the same time to provide a protection from the rather exposed feeling sometimes felt when singing and a way of projecting oneself, of producing sounds that are louder, more dramatic, more expansive and more exotic than the young voice is capable.

Instruments also visualise music in the sense that their design dictates the nature of the music they produce: the layout of a xylophone suggests how it will be played (ascending and descending by step, glissando). They evoke sensations, associations and connections which stimulate the musical imagination and initiate improvisation or composing i.e. the sound of fingers tapping on a drumhead might suggest urgency/tension/rainfall.

Classroom percussion may well be the first (and only) contact many children have with musical instruments, unless they go on to learn outside the classroom. Their experiences, therefore, should be as musically satisfying as possible, and should progress in terms of technical as well as musical expectations.

Encouraging teachers to use instruments

Instruments should be introduced gradually and with thought to organisation and learning outcomes. You might suggest to generalist teachers that they should introduce instruments as part of listening activities and circle games; here the focus is on the recognition and location of different sounds (timbre, pitch, duration, dynamics, texture), stopping and starting, taking turns, combining sounds, imitating, answering, inventing, sequencing, etc., rather than playing technique. The game format will manage the activity for the teacher; children understand the idea of taking turns, responding to signals, offering their own ideas, inventing and breaking 'rules'. Such games should not be competitive, no-one should be 'out' if they make a mistake and there must be room for all levels of ability to take part.

Advise your colleagues that, when they plan to use instruments, they should choose them in advance and decide how they will be distributed: laid out in the centre of the circle, in a crate, on the trolley, on a table away from the children. If every child is to have an instrument invite a few children at a time to collect theirs or hand them out individually. Ensure that, if children are to choose, there is an adequate collection from which to make a choice. If there are not enough instruments children could choose in pairs and take turns.

It may often be more appropriate to have a few children playing instruments at any one time: accompanying a song, echoing rhythm patterns, or improvising. This will allow everyone to hear what individual children are doing, encourage a more refined and balanced ensemble, and provide opportunities for children to listen and learn from each other. This could be organised so that players sit in the centre of the circle: instruments stay put and children move rather than vice versa.

Adopt an agreed rule about keeping instruments quiet whilst activities are being set up or explained; use a visual signal such as an upstretched hand. Be very insistent on real silence when it is asked for as this will reinforce the importance of silence as a 'frame' for music: a sign of readiness and attention.

Although there is usually a correct way of holding and playing instruments the most important instruction to begin with is that they are not toys and that they must be looked after. Allow children time to explore ways of handling and playing the instruments for themselves before showing them. Finding different ways to produce sounds is an important stage of musical exploration. Correct playing emerges from the desire to find the most appropriate sound quality (most resonant, quietest, highest etc.) and to find the most comfortable playing position so that one can play with control over time. As instruments and music become more complex and sophisticated, learning appropriate playing techniques become increasingly relevant. A recent publication 'From Agogo To Xylophone' (Cotton, 1996) provides a guide for primary teachers to playing classroom percussion.

This kind of management of resources seems common sense but teachers may find it difficult to transfer their experience from other subjects. The perception that music is different, difficult and mysterious tends to de-skill teachers; the potential for high levels of noise does not help either.

The concepts of pitch, tonality and harmonic texture seem to be difficult to teach and to understand. Whereas pulse and rhythm, dynamics and speed are all directly related to movement and speech, pitch and relationships between pitches seem to be less tangible and more abstract. Tuned percussion and the keyboard provide visual and controllable means to teach children about pitch relationships and to explore, understand and use scales, modes, drones, ostinati and chords.

Instrumental playing should have a place in all aspects of the curriculum. There is a tendency to see it as predominantly relevant to composing, but playing accompaniments and learning to play pieces composed by others will offer opportunities for focusing on playing technique and provide musical challenges.

Composing

Children are involved with the process of composing when, for instance, they
- explore and experiment with sound,
- invent sound effects to accompany a story or poem,
- select, sequence and organise sounds,
- add an accompaniment to an existing song or piece,

- use words to create rhythmic phrases,
- improvise a song,
- arrange a familiar piece for xylophone and woodblock,
- interpret a graphic score.

Progression in the ability to compose is marked by an increase in:
- control of elements,
- the ability to combine elements to create a coherent whole,
- the ability to sustain and develop a musical idea,
- the ability to create an appropriate musical interpretation of an idea or feeling,
- the ability to communicate and evaluate musical intentions,
- the ability to surprise.

In the earliest stages of creative work children play freely and rather uncritically with sounds. Compositions are transitory, ephemeral and impulsive. As children acquire performing and listening skills they are increasingly able to achieve a considered outcome through experimenting and selecting what they feel is appropriate to the intention. Children's compositions sometimes seem arbitrary, chaotic or fleeting; a piece has too many ideas or too few, it is over in a flash or the same idea is repeated many times. One is always aware of the skill and experience gap between imagination and execution. However, as is often pointed out, we have no difficulty with understanding and tolerating this 'gap' in children's art making or creative writing. At this stage, when composing has been a statutory requirement for six years, teachers are still grappling with the logistics of facilitating the process in the classroom. There has been a feeling that somehow the composing process must not be interfered with: that the teacher should set up the task and then leave well alone, apart from keeping order and monitoring. This is clearly not enough. Teachers need to engage with the process of children composing through listening, questioning and helping to solve problems. Davies in 'Take Note' (1993) suggests some basic questions that the teacher should ask of themselves and the children when composing:

❛ *How long shall I make this idea 'go on'?*
What other ideas will contrast or go with this first idea?
Do I want this to sound louder? Quieter? Faster? Slower?

Do I want to repeat that idea? How many times shall I repeat it?
How can I begin my piece?
How can I extend it?
How can I finish it? How can I change this idea?
Would this sound better on another instrument? . . .

The ability to develop as a composer is nurtured through the experience of composing itself but also through *all* musical experiences both in and out of school. The music children habitually listen to; the music they learn when singing, dancing and playing; the thinking, talking and recording they do when responding to music, all feed their musical imagination and can be exploited in creative music making.

To help your colleagues understand what composing is and what the processes are, you will need to give them practical experience in a workshop setting with other staff, and involve them in composing alongside their own class.

There is no shortage of published teaching materials to provide ideas and frameworks for composing but, for yourself and your colleagues you will still need to become increasingly able to mediate the learning that takes place whilst children compose and to recognise the quality of children's achievements in the outcomes.

Listening and appraising

❜ *Valuing music is the ultimate aim of music education . . . No one can oblige anyone to value anything. But we can make sure that students become skilled and sensitive with a range of materials . . . and we can demonstrate our own valuing by the way we respect and attend to the music of children and others.*

(UCKMET, 1993)

There are two principal concerns here:
1 the need to develop aural skills: learning to recognise, discriminate amongst or analyse musical elements.
   These should develop alongside and as a consequence of performing and composing but can be supported with circle

games, devising or interpreting notations, and listening for specific features or elements in a piece; and

2   the need to provide opportunities for children to experience a range of different musics and for them to explore a variety of ways to respond.

These are not mutually exclusive, in fact, one would hope that either would lead to the other. One of the problems with point 2 is that everyone, including teachers, has strong personal feelings about the music they choose to listen to. This can lead to difficulties when tackling matters of taste and interpretation in the classroom. There is no guarantee that first, the children will be engaged by your choice of music or second, they will interpret what they hear in the same way. To children who are unfamiliar with nineteenth century orchestral music, Mendelssohn's 'Hebridean Overture' may not conjour up images of the sea. If you have planned your lesson on an assumption that they would, you may find that things come unstuck!

Responses can also be coloured by association: TV, adverts and film influence, very powerfully, our interpretations of the music we hear. We need to recognise the force of visual images, and narrative in attributing meaning to music, and either exploit it or consciously counter it. We can use drama, prose, poetry and dance to express the mood or a narrative interpretation of a piece (whether the composer intended this or not); we can use the narrative form to provide a framework for composition. However, it is also important to respond to and work with music, musically. That is, without reference to other art forms. This can be difficult in an educational setting as we, as teachers, have to be concerned with recognising the response: we need some kind of access to what is going on and the typical ways are to talk, to write, to gesture, to make marks or to move. We should also be seeking evidence of the child's response to music through what they show in their own music-making.

One might think of the repertoire as nourishment to feed the imagination, to strengthen understanding, to introduce new, surprising, challenging questions, or interpretations. There needs to be a continuum of experience between children's music and grown-up music: a recognition that the materials are the same, that the fundamental processes and structures are the same, even if the outcomes can seem to occupy different worlds. Recognising what these materials, processes and structures are is the basis of the subject knowledge which teachers need if they are going to teach music.

As the coordinator you will need to help teachers understand that:

- children are involved in the skills of listening and appraising when composing and performing as well as when they are audience-listening
- listening to music can take place in many different learning contexts: to illuminate understanding of other times, places and cultures; to stimulate or enhance creative work in other arts
- children are likely to be more interested in music which resonates with their own experience either of music they have heard before or of ideas and materials they have worked with themselves
- dance is a powerful medium for appraising music
- children's capacity to listen attentively needs to be developed
- it is easier to listen to a new or unfamiliar piece if there is some focus for the listening
- a piece or extract needs to be heard several times (in a session and over several sessions) for the music to be 'known' (remembered, recalled, appreciated, absorbed)
- sometimes we should listen to a piece for no other reason than the experience itself
- as much as possible children should hear whole pieces. Some traditions and styles make this easier than others: popular songs and dance music, folk, and secular early music will tend to be shorter and structurally less complex than 'serious' music. However, there is a lot of classical music other than symphonies and concertos, which can be accommodated: songs, piano pieces, baroque dances, movements from suites, overtures, themes and variations
- any music is suitable as long as you have thought clearly about how you intend to use it and whether it illustrates clearly, for the children, that intention

- it is much easier to listen analytically when the texture is uncomplicated or involves distinctly different instruments or elements. The blended sound of a nineteenth century orchestral piece is much more demanding than the diverse texture of a jazz quintet
- children are far more unprejudiced about music than adults

In this respect you have a responsibility to be constantly on the lookout for recordings which will expand the listening repertoire in school. Certain publications for teachers help with this by offering ideas which arise from less familiar sources (McGregor, 1995; McNichol, 1992; Adams, 1997). Many recording companies now produce inexpensive samplers on CD which introduce short pieces of, say, contemporary music, music from different continents or historical periods. Listen to music programmes on the radio or TV which explore musical styles that are new to you. In these ways you will constantly refresh your own knowledge and have a more diverse range to offer colleagues when they ask for help. The contribution that can be made by live musicians (visiting instrumental teachers, professional groups etc.) should be exploited whenever possible.

A research project at Huddersfield University (Flynn, 1996) has been investigating the nature of appraisal in music with a group of primary teachers. They identified nine areas within which appraising occurs:

> *Pupils appraise music when they:*
> - *listen to music for a particular purpose*
> - *investigate, explore and find out about sound and music*
> - *create something in response to music*
> - *use background research and information to understand what they hear in music*
> - *move to music*
> - *try to achieve an idea which they have already conceived*
> - *choose, select, reject sounds or music*
> - *use prior experience to understand music*
> - *respond verbally to music in questions, opinions, explanations, statements and descriptions.*

Notation

Musical notation has evolved over time, closely allied to the particular musical tradition that it records. All systems arise from an attempt to fix in some visual way the sound and structure of music. As a result they all, to some extent, analyse and record certain musical features. Staff notation can record pitch and rhythm fairly accurately but is not so effective for timbre, dynamics or speed. Graphic notation, which is invented by the composer is better at recording such elements and less orthodox sounds. There is a particularly strong connection between graphic notation and physical gesture: the marks children make in response to sound express their movement response more readily than an analytical one. They draw the upward sweep of a scale or the zigzag movement of a scraping sound. Ways of recording rhythm tend to be quite closely related: separate regular marks to show a steady beat, dots close together for quicker patterns and so on.

Notation in music education can be seen as a valuable teaching aid:

■ we have something visual by which we can draw attention to certain techniques and knowledge, and consolidate understanding
■ we know if something is technically accurate in the performance of a piece from the repertoire, by comparing it to the printed music
■ we can check whether children can hear and and reproduce sound patterns
■ we can ask a child to talk through their score of a composition to explain their intentions
■ we can learn and teach new and unfamiliar repertoire from notated sources
■ we can more readily record, store and analyse children's compositions

Music is a fleeting and ephemeral art form so in a teaching context it is difficult to hold on to what is happening. The difficulty is that for children and inexperienced music makers, notation both in reading and writing, tends to obstruct and slow down the process of making and responding to music. It may also reduce and limit the musical ideas and expression that children might have when communicating their music. People who have learned their music skills through notation may use it as a crutch, are nervous without it and are in danger of using their eyes more than their ears when engaged with music. A balance needs to be found so that we neither subvert the immediacy and imagination of children's music nor exclude them from using useful notation systems.

Teachers will often define their musical abilities by whether they can read traditional notation. It has high status in the western classical tradition because it gives access to musical 'text'. In our culture an educated person is a literate person so the classically trained musician has higher status than the folk or jazz musicians who learn and play by ear. As a literate music teacher it is very difficult (and perhaps hypocritical) to convince your colleagues that knowledge of traditional notation is irrelevant. What is important is that you can persuade them that it is not the starting point for music making and understanding but an aide.

You will need to consider what value you give it and what place it holds in your own practice.

> *Teaching notation needs to have purpose and meaning. It should, in the first instance, arise out of a need that the music-maker identifies. It can have several different purposes:*
>
> - *To help us remember — as an aide-memoire — we may just write down an outline, important moments, or complicated passages*
> - *To communicate our music for others to play; in which case they need to understand our language*
> - *To give everyone a plan (score) of what happens. Each player can see how their part fits into the whole. This is useful for a conductor, if there is one*
> - *To help in the refining and rehearsing process. The composer can 'tinker' with the piece and refer to particular sections in rehearsal. Individual players or groups can take their part away to practice*
> - *To enable the music-makers to experiment and discover different interpretations of the same score . . .*
> - *To give children (in the context of the wider curriculum) an opportunity to explore the nature of visual symbols and their power to communicate meaning* (Hennessy, 1995)

If you feel that it is important for all children to read and write staff notation by the time they leave in Year 6, then who teaches music, what and how they teach will need to serve this aim. If children are to become fluent users of notation then it will need continuous and thorough attention.

If you see value in introducing the basic principles and using them alongside other forms of notation then teachers will be able to use a variety of notations which suit the particular activity. You should also be able to increase their knowledge without too much anxiety. If you decide that only those who are having instrumental lessons should need this skill you may be excluding the majority of children from gaining some insight and understanding which they might find interesting or useful in the future. Even rock and folk musicians will, on occasion, find being able to notate something or learn a new piece from notation useful. For your colleagues who have no experience of notating music, consider a staff inservice session to demonstrate a variety of approaches to notation:

- graphics,
- colours,
- numbers for pitches or beats,
- two-line stave,
- rhythm grids,
- word rhythms,
- taking a pencil for a walk,
- show how the principles of staff notation relate to certain graphic ideas,
- bring some examples of music scores produced by twentieth century composers and children to show how some of the solutions are the same,
- introduce colleagues to a music notation programme for computer which children can use independently.

It clearly states in the National Curriculum documents for all of the UK that, in the primary music curriculum, children should be taught to invent and use notations, be able to respond to symbols and incorporate their understanding into their composing and performing, and to record features of the music they listen to.

Chapter 5   Teaching and learning styles

Music teaching has often been characterised by a rather didactic teaching style: teacher as instructor. When music education was largely aimed at teaching children the skills of singing and playing so that they could perform and, hopefully, come to appreciate our musical 'heritage', there might have been some justification for this approach. Learning *about* the repertoire was also a feature: lives of the great composers, following a score, knowing the story of 'Peter and the Wolf' or identifying the animals in 'Carnival of the Animals'. The principles of staff notation and Italian terms might also be introduced. Where there was no specialist the school radio broadcasts would replace the teacher: teaching songs by rote and playing pieces of music for listening. This is, of course, a somewhat exaggerated picture but I suspect that most readers will recognise some of it from their own schooling.

None of this is necessarily inappropriate but offers a rather limited and limiting musical experience, neglecting the importance of developing musical creativity, which is now a central component of the curriculum. We still have a lot to learn from approaches to learning in other arts subjects and, fortunately, the national curriculum supports this to some extent. The emphasis is now firmly on the child as emerging musician: improvising and inventing alongside skill-building and responding to the music of others.

Children learn through play, imitation, exploration, experimenting, observing and listening. Their motivation to learn is generated by pleasurable experiences, curiosity, a sense of achievement and positive feedback.

It is now more clearly understood that what children learn *through* music is as significant as what is learned *in* music. Music in school is recognised as a social activity, a means of communicating and sharing with others, a way of knowing and understanding ourselves and our relationship with others. Although music can also be a very solitary pursuit it is difficult, although not impossible, for this to be consistently offered to every child in the context of school. Managing and facilitating group work, supporting composition activities and using the repertoire for interactive learning rather than passive listening require rather different teaching skills to those of an instructor.

The consequence of these changes is that teachers of music have had to adopt a variety of teaching styles to reflect the different ways we expect children to learn.

Suggestion

Look at these descriptions of different kinds of teacher and consider your own teaching styles.
Are some more familiar to you than others?
Do you think you use very different teaching styles in music compared with other subjects?
Which styles do you think your colleagues most associate with music teaching?
Which styles do you think are most accessible to your colleagues?

1   The teacher teaches by demonstration, passing on specialist skills and knowledge through direct instruction and controlling every stage of learning through practising, refining and performing. Children perform and respond as instructed and as a whole class but do not contribute ideas to the lesson. All decisions about repertoire, musical interpretation and criteria for evaluation are made by the teacher.

2   The teacher teaches a song or piece to play, by rote (aurally), focusing on particular features of the music: asks questions about mood, structure, 'who would sing this kind of song?', 'when/where would this kind of music be played?' Children learn initially through imitation. But are encouraged to make musical decisions. Children contribute ideas of how expressive elements, such as dynamics and speed, affect the feeling of the music. When teaching different parts of part-song or ensemble piece, everybody learns everything so that musical understanding grows out of shared knowledge and experience. An 'organic' approach is adopted so that at each stage everyone has a grasp of how the different parts relate to each other. Composing and listening activities are initiated and managed by the teacher and may be for whole class, group or individual work.

3   The teacher leads circle games for skill-building: developing quick responses, coordination, maintaining a steady beat, pitch matching, listening. Positive, non-competitive conditions are provided for practise, exploration, improvisation, and whole class involvement. Leadership might change once a game is established so that teacher becomes part of the group; children are, by turn, leader, performer or audience. In this way children learn from each other as much as from the teacher.

4   The teacher offers stimuli and initiates musical activity to generate ideas for creative work. Within a given framework children may work as a whole class, in groups or individually. Outcomes are differentiated and open-ended, everyone contributes to a final composition/event or each composition is heard individually. Teacher supports the children's learning by offering help to solve problems, questioning to challenge ideas, joining in as equal participant. Teacher mediates between the subject knowledge and the children's abilities, and helps children to develop their appraisal skills through questioning and conversation.

In any one lesson or sequence of lessons you are likely to use a combination of these styles. The greater the focus on composing and children's own responses to music the less didactic the teacher needs to become. Teaching music requires the skill of knowing when to intervene in a creative process and when to leave well alone; when to challenge, when to praise, and when to listen. Your colleagues will need a great deal of help with this as it derives very much from first hand experience and recognising, in what they see and hear, the quality of music making that is evident and what the next step might be for any particular child.

Your colleagues should be quite familiar with the role of teacher as facilitator, mediator and monitor from their experience in teaching other subjects, especially in creative, investigative and problem solving tasks. On the other hand, taking on the more formal, whole-class directing-from-the-front approach may be less common. Here the teacher needs to learn the basics of how to rehearse and direct: clear signals for starting and stopping, using hand gestures to shape the performance, keeping everyone in time, improving intonation and controlling dynamics.

Colleagues who do not have experience as music makers themselves are likely to find the director role rather daunting. You will need to find ways of tackling their concerns. Consider:

- Stressing the importance of composing, listening and appraising. Demonstrate how composing fosters performance skills and that children will often find their own solutions to keeping time, starting and stopping and controlling expressive elements.
- Focusing class music on skill building through songs and rhythm work which are linked closely to language and movement.

- Encouraging children themselves to lead activities.
- Providing material on tape: songs or accompaniments and rhythm games.
- Encouraging colleagues to prepare themselves thoroughly when planning to teach a new song or rhythm piece (play the tape repeatedly to know the piece inside out).
- Trying to establish regular mini-workshops for the staff (once or twice a term perhaps) to share new repertoire and to give them the opportunity to air things they find difficult, like starting a song.

Formal conducting should not be necessary for classroom music-making; simple, natural gestures should be enough. To help with their understanding of what to look and listen for it would be worth considering tape recording (video if possible) some examples of activity in *your* class to share with the staff in an INSET session. You can replay and pause to help focus on what's happening and invite colleagues to consider how they might respond to individual children or groups.

Another effective method, though more expensive, is for you to teach a class and suggest that the class teacher either observes the children, observes but participates, or acts as an assistant.

Learning in groups, individually and the whole class

The National Curriculum recommends that children should be 'given opportunities to use sounds and respond to music individually, in pairs, in groups and as a class' (DfE, 1995). When composing became an established part of the curriculum, groupwork quickly became the habitual way of managing creative work in the classroom. Composing in primary music is now almost synonymous with groupwork and it is becoming clear that we need to be rather more thoughtful about its value and efficacy.

Children need to be taught how to work in groups and their ability to work successfully will depend as much on their group working skills as it will on their musical abilities, perhaps more so. These skills go hand in hand with the general developmental factors which lead to becoming socially aware, tolerant, sensitive to the needs of others, able to accommodate the views of others, able to contribute, lead or follow. The ability to cooperate and collaborate will be developed in several contexts and, in particular, in activities which rely on it: team games, discussions, drama, science experiments, design and technology tasks. True groupwork is that in which a group work together to solve a problem, create a piece of work to which all have contributed as a result of collaboration. This is not the same as four children sitting round a table in a group, each doing their own work, even if they are sometimes helping each other.

In music, group composition has rapidly become the norm for a number of reasons:

■ there is not enough space to allow each child a place to compose their own piece
■ there is not enough time to hear each composition during or at the end of the process
■ there are not enough instruments to give each child a selection
■ individually not all children will have the ability to realise their musical ideas either because of their own limited playing abilities or lack of ability in the composing process itself
■ a group allows for more satisfying musical sound in terms of textures and dynamics in particular. Young children will produce limited vocal sound and need the support of a large group
■ even very elementary pieces will have addressed, consciously, issues of structure even if it's only in terms of who plays when
■ greater variety of timbre and pitch will be available
■ a group will be learning about keeping in time, listening, texture, ensemble playing, rehearsal, and apprasisal through having to share the process with others
■ critical listening and sharing language to describe and explain is fostered
■ it makes it possible to focus on the achievements of individual children without needing to pick them out for attention

However, there are several drawbacks to organising music learning in this way:

- in any session children may be left to their own devices for longish periods of time if you are trying to support each group in turn
- unless children are used to groupwork they may not be able to work in a sustained and purposeful way
- composing by committee may, ultimately be frustrating for the individual who has strong ideas of their own
- unless there is very generous accommodation groups will have to work with a lot of noise
- which group gets the bass xylophone?

Whether you have planned for groupwork or not it is important to model the composing activity in some way.

> This way the teachers pass on to the students clear procedural guidance and technical know-how which otherwise can be neglected. There is a danger, of course, of the model being too dominant, but in the first stages it is far better for this to happen than for disorganised work to depress both teacher and the students. An antidote to unwanted dominance lies in the teacher's use of language, for example 'in this situation you might use this or you may choose to do that. If this, then . . .'
>
> (Odam, 1995, p. 76)

Make it clear to colleagues that group work is not always the most appropriate approach: With the youngest children you will probably plan to keep the children together as one group when working with a composing task but offer follow-up opportunities through the provision of a music corner for individual or paired work (see music corners Chapter 14).

- Certain composing tasks may be concerned with arranging some 'given' music (a song, or rhythm patterns, or a chord sequence). The whole class could contribute to the piece with the teacher acting as 'chair' and perhaps director, although with the Y5 and 6 classes certain children should be able to direct.
- The task might involve interpreting a painting, poem or scenes in a drama. In this case there could be a mixture of group and whole class work: groups working for quite short amounts of time and referring back to the class at regular intervals to try out particular ideas and gradually pull it all together as one piece.

- The composing structure might allow for different improvised sections held together by a recurring theme or chorus which the whole class perform. The improvisations might be performed individually or in pairs.
- Consider organising group composing so that in each group there is only one 'composer' who makes the creative decisions. The rest of the group are the performers.

Daphne has been experimenting with this approach with her Year 5 class:

> I have sent the children off in groups but I have identified a composer and I've found that that's been really helpful — for me and the children — because when they come back the composer has to tell me why they chose certain instruments, why they've done certain things, whether they feel its worked or not. Whereas when you've got, say, four children all trying to contribute their own little bit its much more difficult to assess. I've found that even the performance aspect is much better: they play together far better, the control has improved immensely because they're not any more trying to show off 'this is the bit I composed on my instrument'. They're doing it to help the composer and there's far more listening to each other.

When advising colleagues about composition make it clear that there should be a clear structure for the children to use. Whether the outcomes are to be 'open' (divergent, a variety of interpretations) or 'closed' (a predetermined outcome), everyone will need some kind of framework for their ideas: just saying 'go away and make up a piece of sad music' will not be enough for most children. There may be a reluctance to prescribe content or structure when developing musical creativity, but in most creative contexts there is some kind of commissioning constraint (time, resources, purpose, place, technical abilities) and in the classroom one also has learning objectives.

There is a peculiar simultaneous opposing tension in the development of the composer. On the one hand the inexperienced composer needs the freedom to experiment and on the other a clear structure and specific material to work with. Too much choice, too many decisions to make can be just as paralysing as too few. The more experienced composer can be challenged by restrictions (use only one note) or by none.

This means that teachers need to be responsive and flexible in the way they accommodate and facilitate creative work.

Chapter 6   The multicultural classroom

> ❝ *Composers today draw on the full diversity of culture available to them. Those learning should be exposed to practical experience of an equally wide variety of music.*
>
> Boulez in a letter to the *Guardian* (17.2.92)

It is now widely accepted, and enshrined in the National Curriculum, that children should be exposed to a broad and diverse musical repertoire. The educational rationale for this has been well-aired within the music education community as well as amongst educationists as a whole. Music is an expression of collective as well as personal values, beliefs and actions, and what happens in school should reflect, acknowledge and celebrate this.

The imperative to include musical traditions from all over the world in the curriculum arises from two main sources:

1 *Musical:* music is in a state of continual change and development, influenced by the way people live and where they live. The more we are exposed to different musics through recordings and our own travels, the more music will reflect the mixing and fusion of different styles and traditions (Paul Simon's 'Graceland', the compositions of Steve Reich, Gershwin's 'Rhapsody in Blue', The Gypsy Kings, Bhangra and so on). On the other hand, and for the exact same reasons, communities who are displaced or in a

minority seek to maintain their own cultural traditions and their distinctive musical voice.

The National Curriculum describes music in terms of elements and processes which can be readily applied to any music. For instance, if the learning aim of a unit of work is to recognise 'ostinato' and to perform and compose repeating patterns, the teacher might find several listening examples and choose repertoire from a variety of styles or traditions to perform, or from which to draw ideas for composing. In this way unfamiliar musics avoid becoming ghetto-ised or marginalised.

The counter to this is that sometimes a particular style or tradition should be the focus of the learning so that children have the opportunity to listen more closely to its distinctive sound and understand and appreciate its cultural context. Music can, thus, contribute to learning in the humanities and other arts subjects, and vice versa. Experiencing songs in different languages helps to reinforce the relationship between language and music.

Exposing our ears to the unfamiliar should encourage us to appreciate the familiar and challenge our perceptions of what music is and can be.

2 *Social:* understanding breeds tolerance, and in a world where individuals are more mobile with regard to where and how they live and work, schools become important places in which understanding and appreciation of our similarities and differences can be fostered.

Through celebrating festivals, sharing songs, stories and dances, the school grows to value the whole community in which children live:

- Yvonne invited parents to come in to school to teach Gujerati songs to her and the children. She has recorded the songs and they are now an ordinary part of music lessons.
- The Wren Trust work with schools to rediscover or reinvent local traditions such as Well Dressing, May Day celebrations and wassailing.

■ Divali, Eid, Hanukah, Chinese New Year and other festivals are included in assemblies where music is invariably the focus.

As coordinator you have a responsibility to encourage and develop a rich experience of music and, at the same time, to avoid a superficial or tokenistic approach. This is not easy as we are all more or less knowledgable and interested in particular styles. There are several ways to improve your own and your colleagues' knowledge:

■ many recently published resources include well-chosen examples of repertoire from all over the world. There are often supporting notes and activities which give contextual information, and some musical analysis;

■ TV and radio programmes such as The Music Machine (BBC R3) often feature the music of a particular tradition;

■ find out about what goes on in the community and arrange for musicians to perform to the children or run a workshop (the local arts centre or the Regional Arts Association should have a register);

■ invite parents to teach songs, games and traditional dances to the children: if there is a policy of parents helping with reading you may already have some who are happy to do this; and

■ seek out inservice courses which focus on or include work with unfamiliar musics.

There is no shortage of information, instruments or recordings to support a multicultural music curriculum. The difficulty is focused more on educating ourselves in exploiting such resources and making appropriate choices.

A good starting point is to look for children's songs and games from around the world, and folk dance material. Whatever the origin, such music should be accessible and fairly easily learned. Such repertoire should communicate the basic musical elements of that style or tradition in terms of rhythm, melodic shape, scales, texture, timbre and structure. Using stories will also provide a context for introducing the music and dance of that same tradition.

In the past music education has been dominated by
the musical achievements of what is really quite a small
'club': European male composers who lived between 1600
and about 1950. Now that the music curriculum aims to give
children a *practical* and culturally relevant education, we
must be prepared to embrace not only classical music but
all kinds of other musics.

❛ *An avalanche of memory is burying us . . . I don't want our
culture to die, but I don't want to preserve it either. I just want
it to go on. I don't want the river to be frozen. I want it to run.*

Boulez quoted in the *Guardian* (6.2.92)

Chapter 7   Special needs

Children with exceptional ability in music are often well-catered for through instrumental tuition and the extended curriculum, but may find themselves neglected in class lessons. Class teachers can feel intimidated by children with musical expertise and concerned about how to involve them. In the section on consultancy (Chapter 2) and the extended curriculum (Chapter 9) I have made reference to the way these children can be challenged and offered tasks at their level. However, it is not unusual to find that children who are learning to play an instrument are unable to improvise, play by ear or move expressively to music. What happens in the class music lesson should be relevant to their musical needs.

I have listed below specific suggestions concerning children with particular needs.

Further advice is available through the publications listed in the resources section.

Hearing impairment

Provide
- instruments which are very low pitched and resonant — bass bars, drums, ocean drums
- rhythmic movement and speech
- visual reinforcement of pitch shapes

- listening games in which contrasts between sounds are dramatic
- reduced background noise
- paired tasks
- wind instruments such as kazoos (for speech development)

Visual impairment

Provide
- instruments which are brightly coloured or reflect light
- opportunities for dance
- paired tasks
- 3D materials for graphic scores: fabric, string, construction or maths blocks, straws, natural materials

Movement impairment

Provide
- instruments which are easy to grasp: lollipop drums, shakers with fat handles
- instruments which are sensitive to very slight or unfocused movement: bells, bar-chimes, autoharp, shakers, big drums
- dance
- paired tasks

IT has a lot to offer in this context: composing software, keyboards and tape recorders will allow children to work at their own pace, to their ideal volume levels (with headphones) and, in the case of computers and keyboards, with a minimum of performance technique. In 'Making Music Special' by John Childs (1996) there is a very useful description of how to use transducers to amplify sound. They can be attached to almost anything and will offer a greatly expanded palette of sounds.

Problems related to literacy or numeracy often fade into the background in music lessons although you may find that the attendant lack of confidence may sometimes hinder their engagement. Children are invited to invent their own notation and in so doing can investigate signs and symbols, notate patterns and play with the conventions of reading (will the score read from left to right? is everything played at once or line by line?). It is well recognised that singing, rhythm linked to speech, the emphasis on coordinated movement and expression of feelings can offer great scope for building skills and confidence which directly support children with learning difficulties.

Children who demand great amounts of attention in lessons where they struggle, may well find that this attention seeking is not needed in music where performing and composing activities will regularly allow individuals to shine.

Listening and performing activities will also develop concentration, attention span, and controlled movement. The practice of circle games in which everyone takes their turn, eye contact is needed, anyone can lead, and all ideas are shared should help children who find working with others difficult and develop their social skills.

The skills of groupwork, as mentioned earlier, need to be developed within a variety of contexts and all children will need this.

Inevitably there is an emphasis on learning *through* music. The range of ability in performing, composing and appraising music will be as wide as that encompassed by the class as a whole. The resources, activities and conditions which are suggested here are those that we would want to provide for all children: space, quiet, comfort, good quality instruments. If the therapeutic properties of music are remembered, the needs of all children will be provided for.

| *Chapter 8* | IT in the music curriculum |

The applications of information technology in music education are changing and developing rapidly. Teachers are in turns excited and anxious about the possibilities presented. The uses of music technologies in primary school must be seen in the context of children's general musical development and should form a coherent strand of the planning for music.

The Department for Education funded a project which has produced guidelines for music IT in primary schools (Music IT Support Project, 1996). These suggest three areas of activity and give examples to illustrate progression and their relationship to the Programmes of Study in the Orders for schools in England:

- Use and investigate sounds and structures,
- Refine and enhance performance and composition, and
- Extend . . . knowledge of different styles of music.

Out of the eighteen examples, two for each of KS1, KS2 (lower), and KS2 (upper), only three involve the use of music software packages for computer. Many teachers may be under the impression that music IT is almost entirely concerned with this application and it will be very reassuring for specialists and generalists alike to realise that, particularly at primary level, there are many other more relevant and creative applications.

I have identified three principal fields of application. These seem to me to be those which are most relevant to the music curriculum in primary schools.

Computers

Appropriate music education software for primary age children is still fairly thin on the ground. This has a lot to do with how production has developed; small companies and individuals design packages which are not grounded in the field of music education. This means that they do not always reflect a particularly creative or relevant approach to the needs of the child in terms of music learning, or the needs of the teacher in terms of class teaching. Designers are not always in a position to consult widely or trial their products in the field before putting their ideas on the market. Software is relatively expensive, compared to other music resources so that when a teacher, who is inexperienced in the use of music technology, is faced with the choice of a few more instruments or listening materials, and music software, s/he is likely to go for one of the former. The greatest difficulty music technology has in becoming established in primary music is in educating teachers to recognise the real, musical value of the best that is available and to avoid the limiting effects of the worst. With the gradual loss of advisory support and constraints on funding for inservice, this seems to be a difficulty which will not easily be resolved.

A great deal of the material that emanates from music technology creators is heavily influenced by the commercial pop industry. This is where the greatest use and the biggest profits are to be found so it is no surprise, but, as a result, notions of what is relevant and appropriate for the classroom are often superficial and musically unimaginative. The problem for teachers is that they need programmes which address the needs of the curriculum. For instance, there are several programmes which are designed to 'drill' children in learning traditional notation and developing specific aural skills such as repeating a melodic phrase exactly and scoring points accordingly. These are exercises which will have limited value for classroom music. They strike me as unmusical and fairly unappealing except as a closed test of music literacy for those who have already developed the skill.

All too often the computer is seen as an adjunct to the music curriculum, a sophisticated toy, rather than an integral part. Teachers need to be convinced through what they see and hear that the experiences that children have sitting at a computer can support, consolidate and enhance what happens in whole class or group music lessons. As yet, practice and provision is very patchy. It tends to rely on the enthusiasms and expertise of individual teachers who have their own equipment at home or have been fortunate to gain competence through attending a course.

There are different types of programme available:

■ There are a number of composing packages which are based on staff notation. These are useful for children who are already learning to use such notation and will allow them to consolidate their skills. They will also be able to compose melodies, rhythm patterns, drones, ostinati and simple harmony parts. In the hands of a specialist music teacher and children with experience of staff notation such programmes can be useful. Notate (Logotron) is a well established example of this kind of programme.

■ Composition programmes using the 'grid' idea are well established, Compose World (ESP) being one of the earliest and most popular. Here the musical sounds or motifs, whether they are pitched or unpitched, are selected from a bank and then clicked onto the squares of a grid, each square representing a bar or phrase. A whole piece can be constructed and played back. The least imaginative aspect of this is the task of unscrambling the phrases of a well-known tune, although there is some value in the listening and sequencing skills required. The more advanced levels of the programme allow you to compose the motifs and use harmonies.

■ Rhythm Box(EMR) is another widely used programme using a grid-based approach. Here single sounds are placed in the squares which represent a beat or division of a beat. Rhythmic or melodic pieces can be gradually developed through copying, adding new patterns and creating layered textures. At Holdsworthy Primary School, Tony Wade uses this programme throughout the school. By the time the children get to Year 5/6 they are composing and editing quite substantial pieces.

The grid concept is a recognised way of introducing children to reading and recording rhythm patterns away from the computer, so there can be a direct route from whole class rhythm work using body percussion or instruments, to the computer and vice versa. The musical value is in the oportunity it offers individual or groups of children to work with the elements of music in a detailed and discriminating way. Unlike the more holistic experience of improvising or composing live with others, such programmes ask the child to 'construct' a piece sound by sound and to listen, at every moment, to how the piece evolves. It will also give children the opportunity to hear their own ideas performed accurately.

These two approaches are complementary: computer generated or aided composition is not seen as a means of replacing or superseding what takes place in the acoustic, physical world of music in the classroom. It should be seen as a way in which ideas generated in a lesson can be taken a step further in realisation: it can offer a far greater range of timbres than is available through classroom instruments. This is especially true if a keyboard is linked to the computer through MIDI. This will add a greater range and better quality of timbres which will more closely match those that children will be familiar with through the music they listen to outside school (pop music, film and TV soundtracks).

Lurking in many teachers' minds is still, perhaps, the feeling that computer generated sound, ('techno' music) is a bit beyond the pale. This is the next phase of the debate over pop music in schools which raged thirty years ago. Music in school will continue to suffer from such cultural dislocation if teachers choose to ignore the best of what is available.

Other approaches to using computers for early music education are available though not widely used. Research into how children represent sound visually (using graphics and pictures) has lead to a programme in which children can draw on the screen in response to sounds, sound patterns or pieces of music (Music Picture Book by IMPAC). They can, alternatively, realise what they have drawn in sound using a keyboard. The 'picture' then represents their musical idea: the size, colour, density and shape of the picture may be linked to musical elements of dynamics, timbre, texture, and pitch contour, for instance. The picture can then be copied so that the musical idea will be repeated.

This approach is particularly relevant to the way in which curriculum music is taught. In whole class music activities children will be working to produce graphic scores in response to a composition or listening experience (to record their ideas, as a form of analytical listening or as a means of visual expression). They may also compose in response to a graphic score produced by themselves or each other. They may be asked to compose in response to the work of visual artists such as Miro, Klee or Kandinsky (who were particularly interested in the relationship between music and art) or more contemporary artists and photographers. Pattern, contrast, texture, space (silence) may be responded to, explored and manipulated. The use of the computer, again, allows children to take their ideas into another medium and perhaps find greater satisfaction in discovering sounds that closely match what is in their head.

Another source of ideas is recorded sounds from the environment (vocal, instrumental, natural or mechanical) in different contexts (ambiances). These can then be put into the computer, so that familiar sounds can become new timbres to be analysed, manipulated and sequenced.

CD ROM

This is seen as one of the richest areas for development in music education, although there is little available so far. The listening and appraising aspects of musical experience, both understanding and knowledge, would be well served by such a resource through researching instruments, composers, musical traditions and styles. There are obvious links here with learning in humanities, art, dance, drama or English:

- finding out about the musical customs of another time or place,
- gaining a sense of cultural context by listening to the music that was composed in the time of a particular artist or writer,
- comparing the design of instruments from different cultures which share the same characteristics.

Recording

Teachers need to realise the creative potential of using this equipment not only to record finished acoustic compositions or performances but also to be the starting point for composing or the medium for the composition.

With portable machines children can record sounds away from the classroom (nature walks, field trips to historical sites, visits to the seashore) and bring them back to discuss, analyse, sample and use for composing ideas, or creative work in other media.

In the classroom children can record their own music making as a final record of a performance or as part of an appraisal process: to listen to a solo or group performance of a song and discuss how it could be improved, to keep a working record of a composition so that ideas can be accurately recalled from week to week, to record group compositions so that children can listen several times to review their own work. The great advantage of the tape recorder is that an individual or small groups can be engaged in such an activity without being disturbed by or disturbing the rest of the class. Buy the best headphones you can afford, the ones that cause the least 'leakage' of sound, and a splitter box which will allow several headphones to be plugged into the same tape machine.

Ideally, the resources for music should include a good quality tape recorder which is designed for recording music. Many of the small machines in school are made for recording speech and do not have very sensitive microphones or big enough speakers to reproduce a wide range of frequencies and dynamics. A personal recording cassette player (the

Y1/2: Sound walk, children collect sounds around the school and play them back. Discuss differences, similarities: contrast of different places (school kitchen versus middle of the school field; quiet reading time versus break time). Use as basis for composition or listening to a piece of music with clear dynamic contrasts.

Y3/4: Tape recording their own story or poem and adding a soundtrack, incidental music or sound effects.

Y5/6: Composing theme music or advertising jingle on a keyboard and recording it as a soundtrack for their own drama work (which could be videoed).

Y5/6: A Year 4 class make an arrangement of a Christmas carol for singers and instruments. A group of older children then record the performance using a 4-track recorder so that the recording levels on each track can be adjusted to achieve a good balance.

best are the ones that reporters use) with an omni-directional microphone (one that can sit on a flat surface) will work very effectively especially if you then play the tape back through a hi-fi system. Alternatively there are machines specifically designed for school use.

A 4-track tape recorder is like a mini recording studio. It allows you to record individual parts one at a time and gradually build a whole piece in layers (tracks). The recording level of each track can be adjusted to achieve the desired textural balance. These are now used fairly routinely in secondary school music departments and are beginning to find their way into primary schools. They are inevitably more complicated to use but, when mastered, will offer opportunities to control the quality of recording and act as a creative tool for composing. Apart from recording with microphones, other equipment such as a keyboard, computer, another tape recorder or electric guitar can be plugged directly into the 4-track. As a first step to learning more about their potential consider contacting a local secondary, FE or HE institution to find out about them and perhaps arrange for students to lead a project on using the 4-track with your Year 6 children.

Tape recorders are probably the most familiar, accessible and appropriate application of technology that primary teachers can use in music. To introduce their use in music to colleagues you might suggest activities such as those in the 'suggestion' box.

Apart from the use children will make of them in developing their own work they will also, simultaneously, provide the teacher with a record of their progress and achievements both in terms of their music learning and their use of IT.

Keyboards and other hardware

Electronic keyboards are now a standard feature of music resources in most schools. However, they are not always the most flexible or creative instrument that is available. As with computer programmes their design has been dictated by the commercial music world rather than education.

At this early stage of children's musical education there can be a tension between the need to build experience and skills which connect music making with expressive, dynamic action, and the desire to make available resources which reflect the sounds and styles of contemporary music and which circumvent technical difficulties. At the touch of a button one can 'play' complex rhythms or harmonised bass lines with a whole bank of different 'voices' or timbres. Integrating a keyboard into classroom ensemble work is often rather unsatisfactory: the sound can be too dominant and rhythmically too rigid.

To play a keyboard with any degree of fluency it is necessary to learn and practice technique. Unless you decide to make this a significant part of the music curriculum for all children its inclusion as a classroom instrument may become frustrating. Odam in *The Sounding Symbol* (1995) comments on one of the most irritating features: 'manufacturers appear to be unwilling to provide machines in which both the rhythm section and the demonstration programmes (the demo button) can be either isolated or made immobile. Both these things provide teachers with unwanted and unnecessary challenges to good class discipline'.

On the other hand, as a method of providing accompaniment for singing or rhythm activities it can be useful. Teachers and children who have some playing skills may find that, with some practice, they can provide simple chordal accompaniments to songs by using the single finger chord feature and following the guitar chords which are often included in published song material. A rhythm pattern generated by the keyboard could provide the steady beat for pulse and rhythm work. As mentioned earlier, a MIDI keyboard will allow you to connect it to a computer, greatly enhancing the available bank of timbres. There are also keyboards with built-in sequencers which enable you to compose and record.

Musical limitations may be outweighed by its motivating potential. Children who are uninterested in acoustic instruments may be much more inclined to become musically active when offered a keyboard or other electronic instruments such as sequencers or drum-machiners. It may also motivate a teacher by making them feel more secure.

Rob supports his colleagues through the use of IT:

> we have two keyboards and a digital piano which I've bought a sequencer for with a computer disk so that I or another piano player can play the accompaniments to songs into it and then teachers have a bank of songs on disk to use with their class. The nice thing is that you can go straight to the track you want like a CD player, alter the speed and transpose. We had an assembly last year when three classes did a performance of 'Joseph' — each class did a bit and it was wonderful because a child operated the digital piano and one of the teachers conducted all the children. You get over the constraints of not having a pianist available.

Drum machines

The **drum machine** is another piece of equipment which might be worth considering. It is a small box which is linked to an amplifier or headphones. The percussion sounds are sampled rather than synthesised and are therefore of much better quality than those found on software. Rhythm patterns can be composed either using real time, where they are tapped into the machine as though it is being played, or step time where the rhythm is plotted on a grid sound by sound (as described for Rhythm Box).

Tony Wade uses a 4-track tape recorder with his Year 5 and Year 6 classes to give children the opportunity to build pieces track by track and appraise the results. He uses a drum machine to overcome the technical difficulties of some kinds of rhythm work. Here he describes its use in a Samba project:

> We started with the taped piece because I wanted them to move and to clap out the rhythm patterns and pick out instruments. The one thing we did do which might have got round the frustrations of not being able to manage the more complex rhythms was to put the patterns on a drum machine at the end of the project. Of course, I said 'live performance is always best but none of us are brilliant rhythm players', and the thing about this machine is that it will faithfully reproduce over and over again at any speed you want it to be. So each child took it in turns, they worked on it in groups to put their patterns down, they had to 'real-time' record it. That was a good activity in itself because they searched through the 48 sounds on the drum machine and tried to find one that sounded as close as possible to the instrument they were playing.
>
> We didn't try combining live and machine because I think it's really hard to match. It's like trying to practise with a metronome, it's just so rigid that I think once you move into that, that has to become the piece of music rather then trying to link it in with live playing.

> The one thing we did do which was nice was to be able to go from one group's pattern to another on the drum machine. You could then just hear how they contrasted, and all of those things you can just dial in the next pattern and it moves without a gap, so that was good to hear and talk about the differences.

He has also used the step-time method when working with some of the more simple West African drum patterns which can be notated using a grid. Children plotted their own patterns on paper then transferred them onto the drum machine to hear an accurate and up to speed performance.

Individual needs

The use of music technologies will also support the need for differentiated experiences. One of the most difficult aspects of the music curriculum for teachers to provide for is the opportunity for children to work individually. Although a lot of work in IT is done in groups using computers and tape recorders it is well suited to solo work. Headphones mean that such work can happen without distraction. The best programmes will provide basic activities for those who need to have time to consolidate simple understandings about the properties of sound and combining sounds, and will also give the most able children a chance to experiment and take activities started in the classroom much further.

> *Where micro-technology is especially powerful is in the possib-ility of giving greater autonomy to each student. . . . there is an imperative for face-to-face interaction, where people can see, hear and respond to one another. . . . Information technology extends and amplifies the possibilities of making direct musical impact; it gives us decent bass-lines, sets of chords, a vast spec-trum of tonal colour, the possibility of shaping ideas directly. It may be that technological progress releases teachers from a fair amount of drudgery — and let us hope students too — leaving us free to use time for other purposes, creating lively events in which people can share in musical discourse con-vivially. Music is a social art.* (Swanwick, 1995)

In your role as coordinator/consultant you may find that music technology is the route to certain colleagues' interest and involvement. A teacher who feels very comfortable with computers and is knowledgable may find tackling music partly through IT far less worrying than asking them to sing or manage percussion instruments. You might introduce music links to work in other subjects (grids-number; properties of sound — science, design technology; researching musical instruments — history etc.). If music technology is not an area *you* feel confident in it will give your colleague something they can offer as a strength. The reciprocal nature of consultancy amongst peers will then be fostered.

Suggestion

- Discuss with the IT coordinator some joint INSET sessions for colleagues to explore IT for music.
- Put in a joint bid for more resources.
- In your audit of music provision include a review of music technology resources in the school, who uses them and how.
- Look at your teaching plans for music and note the activities in which children use or could use a tape recorder.
- Discuss with colleagues the use of CDROM music resources as an integral part of a humanities topic or a science topic on sound.
- Focus on the possibility of planning for more individual work in music using IT.
- Find out what the nearest secondary school has in the way of equipment and whether it could be borrowed or you could take a class to the school to use it. Suggest GCSE or A level music students run a session.

Chapter 9

Providing for instrumental learning

> ❝ *Many people, both within and outside education, are unaware of the gulf that exists between class music and instrumental learning. The impression persists of music in schools as being largely concerned with the development and promotion of instrumental ensembles and choirs . . . Moreover, on public occasions it is largely these choirs, orchestras and music groups which are displayed and represent music education.* (MANA, 1995)

For specialist music teachers in all schools this part of the curriculum can provide enormous potential for musical enjoyment, excellence and challenge. It is also complex and time consuming to manage and maintain; no other subject coordinator is expected to administer and monitor the work of a team of visiting teachers who contribute regularly and significantly to the life of the school. The onus is very much on the coordinator to facilitate and integrate the work of peripatetic music teachers into the school. Increasingly, such teachers are stretched to the limit in terms of travelling and work loads now that central funding has ceased (see below), therefore it is important that arrangements are well thought-out for all concerned. It is easy for visiting teachers to feel rather isolated and uncared for as they rush from school to school snatching brief discussions with co-ordinators, coping with timetable changes and teaching in often less than ideal spaces.

Where the teachers are working for a well established agency or consortium they are likely to have their own published guidelines for negotiations and procedures in school. These may include methods of payment, length of lessons, teaching styles and group sizes, selection procedures and assessment schemes. However, you may also be dealing with individual teachers who are working independently and who may need all these matters discussed and agreed. In this section I will attempt to raise questions and provide information and guidance for this aspect of your responsibilities.

Recent developments

The quality and quantity of provision in instrumental teaching in schools is as varied as all other aspects of the music curriculum.

During the 1970s and 80s virtually all LEAs throughout the UK provided instrumental tuition (Cleave and Dust, 1989); in most cases this was centrally funded and free for all children. The management of the service varied from authority to authority but certain features were common: the vast majority of teachers taught orchestral strings followed by woodwind and brass. Guitar, percussion keyboard, voice and non-western instruments only made up about 16 per cent of total provision. This clearly demonstrates a significant aim of the service which has been (and remains) to produce instrumentalists who can play in a conventional symphony orchestra. Consequently most services also provided a structure of ensembles, bands and orchestras which offer a progressive path to a youth orchestra from which the 'cream' might then graduate to professional training. Wind, brass and jazz bands also provided opportunities for the more able students to excel. In many parts of the country these centrally organised activities continue.

Where a school had established a tradition of instrumental teaching the provision would be continuing and developing. Where a school had no staff able or willing to take responsibility for setting up and running a scheme there would be continuing neglect. Small schools, those in rural areas or disadvantaged communities might also be neglected unless an active policy to draw them in was adopted by the service.

A variety of solutions to the problem of providing equal opportunities for interested children, regardless of where they attended school, were found: after school music centres or Saturday morning classes, secondary schools acting as a centre for a family or cluster of schools, or teams of instrumental teachers serving the needs of one particular area of a county or city. Many of these schemes operated successfully but relied on a generous level of central funding and often still favoured children who had access to private transport.

Since the introduction of Local Management of Schools and the consequent devolvement of LEA funds this situation might be expected to have worsened. Fortunately, and perhaps surprisingly, research shows that in many areas there has been an increase in take-up (Coopers and Lybrand and Mori in Sharp, 1995). There is no conclusive evidence yet, but it seems likely that this kind of provision will increasingly favour the better-off unless government policy is developed to guard against this. In recent years various pieces of legislation have affected provision:

- Although performing music is included as a statutory part of the National Curriculum, instrumental tuition is non-statutory.
- Schools are allowed to charge tuition fees for pupils in groups of up to four. In practice many schools are unable to comply with this ruling because of financial constraints and may be charging for larger groups.
- The introduction of Local Management of Schools (LMS) devolved the vast majority of centrally held funds to schools. This means that individual schools have the responsibility of deciding how much should be ear-marked for instrumental tuition. The coordinator for music is a crucial voice in such decisions. You may need to fight your corner strongly in the face of other bids especially when up against SEN support or the leaking roof.

Where traditional providers have disappeared in some areas, new services have been established. Some 'old' LEA music services have reinvented themselves as trusts or companies but there are also entirely new agencies appearing. Some of these may be aiming to widen the net in terms of what they can offer: classroom support, inservice courses, music tuition in a wide variety of styles and traditions which have not been offered before, and the involvement of professional performers and composers.

There are also individual private teachers who may well be able to offer a cheaper rate or the ability to work more flexibly in terms of the timetable; they may offer particular expertise otherwise unavailable. In this case it is wise to ask for a CV and references and perhaps suggest a trial period before any long term commitment is made.

Instrumental services now have to respond to what parents and children want rather than dictating what is offered. The cost of purchasing instruments, the technical challenge they present, their size and their appeal all contribute to choice. Flutes and clarinets are now much more popular than orchestral strings; keyboard and guitar are also increasingly popular. The loss of a centrally funded service makes it virtually impossible for any real strategic planning to take place in order to ensure that minority interests, both in terms of instruments and musical styles, are met. While the transition from the old order to the new unregulated provision continues we need to be mindful of the long term effects the latter may have.

All this means that there are likely to be many decisions to be made concerning the provision in your school especially where you want to establish or develop it. You need to have thought carefully, sought impartial advice and consulted the school's management body before going ahead with any plans to establish or expand provision.

Some questions need to be addressed to help formulate a policy which will ensure equity, good quality teaching and a coherent enhancement of the music curriculum.

Why should children be offered this opportunity when only a relatively small number will be able to take it up?

The answer to this question should be included in the music policy for the school. Instrumental tuition provides a unique and important means through which children can develop their musical interests.

It should also offer the opportunity for individual abilities to be nurtured and stretched. If tuition is offered on the instruments and music of different cultural traditions, apart from the more usual orchestral instruments, it will give them respect, value and status within the school community. This should be of particular relevance in schools where there are children from different cultural backgrounds.

Certain performance traditions demand a high degree of technical mastery which is difficult to acquire without specialist teaching. However it should be remembered that not all instrumental tuition need be of this kind; recorder, guitar (not classical), keyboard and percussion also offer children the opportunity to extend their instrumental performance skills. These are often taught in larger or whole class groups by school-based teachers (see Chapter 10).

There is no denying that music-making of all kinds, and of good quality, enhances the ethos of a school. This, of course, can be over-exploited by schools eager to promote their image. Coordinators need to be aware of the dangers of undue emphasis on public musical performance and extra-curricular activity. The energy and resources needed to sustain these may well be at the expense of the curriculum entitlement of all children. It can also lead to music being often at the service of other subject areas or events. A balance needs to be struck between offering extension activities to the more musically able and interested, and what is offered to all children through general class music. Whenever and wherever possible the music that children perform should be result of a process through which children have learned, not a 'notebashing' exercise. The audit exercise (Chapter 3) should help to identify any undue bias in provision.

 Learning in and through instrumental music opens the door for young people to nurture:
- *a love and understanding of music*
- *a wide range of individual skills (reading, technical, inter-pretative, communicative, physical, critical)*
- *sensitive and imaginative response*
- *self-confidence, self-respect, self-reliance and self-expression*

- *co-operation, commitment, team-work, interdependence and loyalty*
- *a sense of discipline, initiative, purpose and achievement*
- *the ability to concentrate on and coordinate several tasks at once*
- *an empathy towards the working of the creative process in other arts* (MANA, 1995)

What will the policy be on charging?

A policy on what to charge parents for lessons is vital. It needs to be seen to be reasonable and fair by all concerned. It may be that where the majority of children in the school have no means of paying this might lead to a different decision about what kinds of instrumental playing opportunities should be offered. Keyboards, guitar, recorder and classroom percussion might all be within the scope of what staff can teach. Special funding for one-off projects to introduce whole classes to instrumental music skills may be possible. Investigate Lottery funding (see pp. 174–5) which might be able to finance the purchase of instruments and/or the costs of a teacher, especially if you include community use or involvement. Consider Samba, Steel Band or Gamelan workshops.

Otherwise, you will need to work out the costs of tuition based on an hourly rate for the visiting teacher, the number of children in a teaching group and the length of lesson. As LEAs gradually reduce the level of subsidy to their 'in-house' provider, the cost to schools will rise. Devon Youth Music (DYM) at present charge a subsidised rate to schools of £20.16 per hour. It is estimated that once the LEA subsidy disappears this cost will rise to around £26. In their Prospectus for 1996/97 DYM present a number of examples of how a primary school might calculate costs to parents:

Example 1
200 pupils on roll with 20 currently in the scheme. Tuition in small groups.
Average of 3 pupils per 1/2 hour tuition @ £20.16 per hour.
Agreed charge of £35 per term, with 5 pupils on 50% remission

Cost of tuition	115 hours tuition = 3.5 hours per week @ £20.16	£2318.40
Income from parents	15 × £35 + 5 × £17.50 × 3 terms	£1837.50
Funding required from School Budget Share		£480.90

Example 2

200 pupils on roll with 20 currently in the scheme. Tuition in small groups.
Average of 4 pupils per hour tuition @ £20.16 per hour.
Agreed charge of £40 per term with 6 pupils on 60% remission

Cost of tuition	99 hours tuition = 3 hours per week @ £20.16	£1995.84
Income from parents	14 × £40 × 3 terms + 6 × £18 × 3 terms	£2004.00
Funding required from School Budget Share		NIL

(Source: Devon Youth Music)

It needs to be understood that in parts of the country where there is not a large pool of professional musicians the majority of teaching will be undertaken by teachers whose sole income is found in this way. Where possible they will want full-time employment and this can be gained through such providers. As a result costs will be higher than that charged for a freelance professional who teaches to supplement other professional work and is paid an hourly rate. Ironically costs in large cities where professional musicians live and work may be lower than in the rural counties.

You will need to decide, in consultation with the head and governors, whether the school is able, or should, subsidise children whose parents are receiving income support, or perhaps have more than one child learning in the school (this is what DYM suggest). Sadly, it is very unlikely that you can give lessons to all the children who want them.

Louise, the coordinator in a small middle school, describes her responsibilities. She has been in post for three years and this is her first appointment since qualifying.

Until this year where I'm more on top of it, it has been one of the hardest parts of the job: sorting out which children want to learn what instrument and what level they are, sorting out the costings. Devon Youth Music (DYM) send a brochure which sets out guidelines on size of groups, what tuition is offered, length of lessons but I had to make all the decisions. In some ways the school is just the go -between between the parents and children, and DYM. I have to come up with a fee that is reasonable; at the moment no child pays more than £39 per term. All children learn in groups so to prevent a child dropping out after a term and leaving the others having to pay more we have to insist that parents sign up for the whole year. This is difficult because beginners often want to just try it out and may not want to continue, but it's the only way we can cover the costs at the moment. If a family have more than one child learning them the cost is halved for the second child, parents on income support also get this subsidised rate. Fortunately we only have a few like this, if there were many more I don't think the school could afford it. Having to pay up for a year also puts some parents off: we have 40 children learning at present and I guess we'd have another 25 if money wasn't a problem.

> We send out letters in the summer term asking if there is interest in learning an instrument and in September I probably spend the equivalent of 8 full working days sorting it all out. Parents are supposed to be responsible for getting an instrument for their child. Most of them hire and I usually find myself dealing with a lot of phone calls and queries about this. DYM do all the assessment of the children, they have practice diaries which are signed by parents and the teacher. They also do reports for parents and advise them on how to support their child's learning. I think they have an appraisal scheme for the teachers as well. Occasionally I sit in on a lesson but usually only when a parent has rung up with some concern.
>
> The music in school definitely benefits from having so many children learning but I do find it a very time consuming job; it's taken a long time to learn how to do it.

Yvonne is the music coordinator for a primary school with 700 children, the vast majority of whom are Asian Indian. Music and the other arts have been highly valued and about £4000 per year is spent on providing instrumental tuition to around 60 KS2 children.

Tuition is provided by teachers from the Leicestershire instrumental service. They teach harmonium, keyboard, tabla, santoor, violin and sitar. Parents pay £1 per lesson and instruments are provided by the school. To support practise an ancillary is paid to supervise lunchtime sessions. Children make good progress playing in concerts and festivals both in and out of school; many continue at secondary school.

Yvonne's problem is that there is now a newly appointed headteacher who wants to prioritise other subject areas (English and maths in particular). She thinks it is likely that the subsidy will diminish and parents will not be able or willing to pay more.

Rob is the coordinator in a very large primary school with over 600 children. This is his first appointment and he has been in post for five years taking over as coordinator three years ago. The instrumental teaching provision is administered quite differently here:

> I'm very fortunate because with the instrumental lessons the majority of the administration, including the finances, is done by the school secretary. It's still a total nightmare to sort out. Because of problems with the quality of organisation. I know of a secondary music teacher, along with some other schools in the area, who is thinking of finding teachers elsewhere. The problem is that the teachers who work for DYM are vetted whereas independent providers and teachers would not be, so it would be difficult to guarantee consistent quality. There would also be a problem of finding other teachers to cover all instruments.
>
> We've cut down on the numbers of children learning and lessons now take place after school to avoid children missing other subject lessons.

Philip is the headteacher and music coordinator of a medium-sized primary school.

> About 60 out of 300 children learn instruments through the school, but there are many more having private recorder or guitar. At least a third of the children are involved in instrumental learning. We don't have a choir, everybody sings. But we do have an orchestra. Tuition is partly provided by Oxfordshire and also by a commercial firm called Normans. Payments are made directly by parents to the firm, we just provide the facilities. All lessons happen during school time. Class teachers have traditionally viewed children having lessons as an inconvenience and an annoyance. I have questioned that all along — because we have a policy that talks about helping able children and enthusiastic children. I don't think they can have their cake and eat it; either they agree with that policy of enabling or they don't. All I try and do is say to the classteachers 'if these children are coming out at inconvenient times you need to go and negotiate with the instrumental teacher'. But there's no doubt that my colleagues have been irritated by me and the system.
>
> It costs parents between £40 and £50 per term depending on which service they are buying.
>
> We do orchestra sectional practices on Tuesday mornings at 8.30. A parent comes in to take the strings and I take brass, woodwind and percussion.

Suggestion

Try to find friends and musician acquaintances (or the visiting teacher) who can help you to acquire some basic skills in instrument maintenance:

violin/cello — replacing strings, setting a bridge, replacing a tailpiece

brass — cleaning and lubricating valves and slides

woodwind — minor action adjustments

guitar — replacing strings and machine heads.

You will also need the names of local suppliers and repairers.

How will instruments be provided?

Evidence suggests that it is the cost of hiring or buying instruments on top of lessons that often discourages many parents. There is no simple answer to this, but consider:

- contacting the local secondary schools or FE college to find out whether they have a store of unused instruments (string and brass instruments may well emerge!). It may be perfectly feasible to arrange a long term loan with insurance cover. You might point out that string instruments deteriorate quite rapidly if not played!
- a lottery grant (find out details from your regional arts association)
- educational or music charities and trusts (often locally based)
- a fund-raising campaign

Another cost is tutor books and sheet music. For multiple copies try to negotiate a discount with a music shop or direct from the publisher, and buy in bulk to sell to children. Remember that photocopying all sheet music is illegal (unless exempt), including hand written copies (Chapter 16).

Finally there is the cost of examinations (Associated Board, Guildhall, Trinity etc.). Certain teachers are very keen to encourage children to take regular exams, and this can lead to parents and children believing that they are an inevitable part of learning an instrument. They are costly, often limited in their ability to assess musical progress, and sometimes counterproductive. Make sure you know what your visiting teacher's approach to examinations is, and make sure that parents are clear about their efficacy. Teachers should not use exams to structure their teaching and most well-run organisations would not encourage such practice.

How will you select children?

It is likely that you will have more children wanting to learn than you are able to provide for. Although, in theory, all those who can pay can play it is still the case that in many schools places will be limited. The main criteria for suitability to learning an instrument should be

- evidence of a strong desire to learn
- evidence of general musical responsiveness (in class lessons: listening or moving to music, communicating ideas or feelings about music).

In most schools instrumental tuition is offered from Year 3 or 4. The general view seems to be the earlier the better for string players but woodwind and brass a year or so later when children's lungs and hands are bigger. Physical size is usually only a temporary problem as children grow fast.

Some teachers take children through aural tests as a means of selecting. Evidence suggests that they have minimal effectiveness and many children who are keen and potentially able, may fail to perform in this context. It is hoped that you will be able to collect enough evidence from the child's class teacher and your own questioning and observations to judge whether s/he is likely to persevere.

There may be a tendency for some gender bias towards certain instruments. Research has shown that certain instruments appear to suggest masculine or feminine traits (O'Neill and Boulton, 1996) and that children may be more attracted to certain instruments because of this. I suspect that there are a number of contributing factors apart from this one:

- certain instruments are considered 'uncool' to be seen with because of the musical traditions they are associated with e.g. stringed instruments = classical
- children may give up if they are bullied or teased by other children
- clarinet, saxophone, guitar, keyboard, drums are associated with pop music and are therefore 'OK'
- some instruments are too big to carry easily, need transporting and take up too much space at home
- some are too loud for the neighbours
- some are too expensive
- on certain instruments progress in the early stages can be quite rapid and rewarding whereas on others it can take take a long time to produce a tolerable tune (violin).

Role models are also a significant influence on children's choice of instrument. Try to arrange for instrumental teachers, professional or good amateur musicians (music students from secondary, further or higher education) to come into school to play to the children and talk about their own learning experience. Women playing brass instruments or percussion, men playing upper woodwind or strings will counter the stereotypical image that may be present. It is recognised that progress and motivation depend greatly on the encouragement and support of parents and teachers, particularly the former. In some respects, when a child begins to learn an instrument their whole family is committing itself to this journey, not only financially but also in terms of aural tolerance and emotional support.

When you approach parents with an invitation to their child to learn an instrument you need to offer some advice and guidance. You might arrange a concert/meeting for interested parents and their children at which the instruments can be heard played by children already learning. You could also give a short talk on the best ways to help their child practise and to motivate them:

- practise should be little and often (10–20 minutes at first),
- try to make time and space regularly available,
- listen to their practise and be positive,
- attend concerts they are playing in.

Alternatively you could prepare a leaflet which sets all this out — keep it light, even humourous (children could help to design and write it) to encourage parents' involvement.

Who will teach and what teaching styles should be adopted?

❛ *Instrumental teachers who visit primary schools usually have qualifications in music, but sometimes insufficient expertise in the full range of instruments that they attempt to teach. The curriculum that they teach is often unduly narrow, and focuses on playing from staff notation, which is not a requirement of the National Curriculum.* (OFSTED, 1995)

There are still too many cases where going to a group lesson means joining a queue for an individual lesson.

(Janet Mills, HMI for Music, in an interview for the Yamaha Education Supplement no.25, 1996)

To play the music of particular traditions there are traditional teaching methods associated with them. The classical music of Europe has been associated with particular teaching and learning styles. These involve a 'master/apprentice' model of teaching which is quite formal and didactic. The learner will expect to attend lessons for many years acquiring the techniques and musical understanding necessary to play music already composed. Folk and pop musicians traditionally learn to play by listening, joining in and perhaps having a few lessons from a friend or fellow musician, the aim being that they develop the ability to play by ear, improvise and accompany others, and, in the case of pop music, hopefully compose their own material. Jazz musicians tend to overlap with both these groups and may have a mixture of formal, classical training as well as developing their own particular style of playing through listening, improvising and 'jamming'. Of course, in practice the boundaries are not so fixed although the classical learner is less likely than others to be encouraged or expected to play by ear, improvise or compose their own music.

Fortunately, the divisions between different styles and traditions are beginning to blur and teachers of classical music are being encouraged to adopt a more flexible teaching style. With the need to take on more group teaching, instrumental teachers are adopting the teaching styles associated with the workshop: playing by ear, improvising, pupil-to-pupil interaction, peer teaching. Notation might make an appearance after a whole term's lessons so that basic playing techniques have become established.

The advent of GCSE and increasing attention given to composing in the curriculum generally, has encouraged (perhaps also put pressure on) instrumental teachers to broaden the scope of their repertoire as well as an awareness of the distinction between the notion of *education* as opposed to *training*. Class music teachers should consider their peripatetic teachers as a rich source of specialist expertise which may be exploited for the benefit of all children not only the small number having tuition.

Most instrumental teachers will expect to teach beginners in groups of about four to six. There are practical as well as good educational reasons for this. Children learn from each other and will develop their ability to listen critically, share and take part in an ensemble right from the beginning. The one-to-one teaching style is expensive and perhaps daunting for the child, with the unalleviated attention of the teacher on the pupil. Within a group lesson there is more opportunity to adopt a variety of teaching and learning styles which will allow experimentation, improvisation, technical training and musical interpretation to be undertaken in an unthreatening situation. The MANA publication referred to earlier suggests a checklist of styles, some of which might be used within the context of one lesson:

> *Command style* — *teacher directed*
> *Practise style* — *allowing passages to be practised*
> *Reciprocal style* — *working cooperatively*
> *Self-check style* — *improving own performance*
> *Guided discovery style* — *teacher leading step by step via questions and demonstration*
> *Divergent style* — *open-ended tasks enabling individual ideas to be developed*

As individual children progress at differing rates it may be necessary after the first year or two to review the groupings. Obviously there will then be the added problem of whether the school and/or the parent can afford to pay an increased fee for their child to have an individual lesson. At one school, if this happens children have to learn outside school hours. The whole cost is borne by the parents although they usually retain the same teacher.

If you are employing teachers independently of an outside agency then you need to find out what their approach to group teaching is. Many 'private' teachers may have had little tuition themselves in how to teach and may model their style on the way they were taught. This may perpetuate a rather didactic and narrowly focused approach which could sit uncomfortably alongside the rest of the pupils' experience of learning in school. Fortunately, there are now a number of initiatives aimed at improving instrumental teaching especially within the private sector. Trinity College of Music, the Associated Board of the Royal Schools of Music, the University of Reading with the Incorporated Society of Musicians all offer courses and qualifications. Teachers who have attended courses such as these should be able to offer well-planned, relevant and rigorous lessons. They should also have a good understanding of what happens in classroom music lessons and be able to contribute where possible.

Consider using visiting teachers in a variety of ways. If there are a lot of staff who feel anxious about their abilities to teach music it will be impossible for you to give all the support that is needed. Visiting specialists might be able to contribute their expertise to certain aspects of curriculum music for certain units of work or topics: listening and appraising experience will be greatly enhanced by live performance, close contact with instruments, talks or workshops led by a specialist performer; children's compositions or arrangements could be worked on and performed with the advanced performance skills of such a teacher. Instrumental teachers will also have the skills to take on the rehearsing and directing of ensembles.

If you want to pursue any of these you will, of course, have to finance this from school funds rather than parental contributions. Providers are aware of the need to diversify what they offer and may well offer packages which include such possibilities.

Where and when will lessons take place?

The children are organised into groups, the teachers are ready to teach them and parents are ready to support them; now you need to work out timetabling and accommodation. The latter will be dependent on the former so discuss with the visiting teachers when they are available and look at appropriate spaces free at those times. The important thing about the space should be that

- it is big enough to accommodate children with instruments, music stands and the teacher
- it is in a fairly quiet part of the school
- it will be undisturbed
- a piano is probably unnecessary although you may provide a keyboard.

You will need to raise this with your colleagues to make sure that everyone understands the requirements and will acknowledge them. When lessons happen can be problematic; many teachers are understandably reluctant to let children leave other lessons. It depends partly on the numbers involved whether this is difficult and you will need to devise a system which disrupts as little as possible. Although difficult to establish, if there are several groups taught in a morning, for instance, these could be rotated so that children do not miss the same lesson every time. Some schools, where the vast majority of children live in the immediate catchment, have the lessons after school. This is very much a whole school issue and if the school wants to include instrumental tuition in what it offers then some compromises will need to be made.

How will you evaluate and assess children's learning?

Music teachers would probably consider performance skills the easiest and most familiar aspect of assessing music learning. It has a long history, through the work of the Associated Board Music examination system which began in the late nineteenth century.

If your visiting teachers are employed by an established agency they are likely to provide some formal method of assessment themselves. Instrumental teaching in schools is included in the inspection process so they are expected to be accountable for the quality of provision. Assessment should be continuous and easily shared between teacher, child, parent and the school.

As an example, Devon Youth Music have produced a 'Pupil Practise Record' book which sets guidelines for practising and criteria for assessment. Pupil and teacher keep a weekly record to show how much practise has been done and to evaluate progress. (See Figure 9.1) (Devon County Council Education). A formal report is provided for parents at the end of the school year. This uses the same criteria and grading system as the record book.

A diary or journal could be produced in which the teacher, with the pupil, sets out learning aims for the term or year, records each lesson with comments and guidance for practise, and writes a brief report on progress at agreed times in the year. This could be at the end of each term for beginners or twice a year for more established players; or it could coincide with the general school reporting cycle. Alongside the teacher's report the pupil should be asked to write a self assessment. As coordinator you should also have access to such reports so that reference can be made to progress and achievement in the school's report.

Assessment should be formative and written in language which is easily understood by everyone concerned.

Apart from such formal methods it should also be possible to monitor progress through children's involvement in class music and performing groups such as the school orchestra. This links with the next question:

How will you motivate these pupils and integrate their emerging skills with the musical life of the school as a whole?

Criteria for Assessment

A) Pupils will have shown an excellent level of understanding, worked with flair and imagination and displayed a mature approach to learning. Tasks will have been completed in a well organised manner with due attention given to accuracy and style.

B) Pupils will have made good progress and demonstrated signs of competence and ability. Interest will have been shown and pupils will have been motivated to complete tasks with some success. Attention will have been given to fluency and technical accuracy.

C) Pupils will have attempted to improve and made some developments. They will have coped reasonably and produced work in a fairly organised manner. Sometimes pupils may be distracted or not always fully apply themselves to set tasks.

D) Pupils will have shown a limited understanding and although basic attempts may have been made to produce results, these will have been done with difficulty. Pupils may lack motivation or have shown little interest.

FIG 9.1
Pupil practice record

Practise Record

Date ....

Notes:–

	Daily Total
Monday	
Tuesday	
Wednesday	
Thursday	
Friday	
Saturday	
Sunday	

Weekly Total	

Pupil Evaluation:

A ☐   B ☐   C ☐   D ☐

Teacher Evaluation:

A ☐   B ☐   C ☐   D ☐

Comments:

Signed pupil ....

(Source: Devon Youth Music, Devon County Council Education)

It is very easy for children who are learning instruments
to form the impression that what they learn in this context
is 'real' music and the class music lessons are somehow
unrelated and irrelevant. 'Real' music is music notated in
books and emulates 'grown-up' music, class music seems to
lack this conventional discipline. This goes back, partly, to
your choice of instrumental teaching staff. If they understand
how what they do connects with what you do (and vice versa,
of course) then there is less danger of this happening.

In your own planning and your support of other class teachers
differentiation should encompass such specialist skills. This
is not easy for generalists although once they realise what
an asset such children can be: playing the melody line of a
song, identifying the starting note from notation, helping with
arrangements of accompaniments, they may be be less
anxious about their presence. Deciding on the makeup of
groups when setting up composing or performing tasks also
needs advice. As with other subjects you need to provide a
mixture of approaches: sometimes you might put those learning
instruments in one group to give them a particular musical
challenge (arranging a notated piece, improvising with a given
pitch set, devising an accompaniment for a song that others
will perform). Equally these children will learn a lot by
working with groups of mixed conventional musical ability.
I use the word 'conventional' because there are bound to be
many other children with musical ability or potential who are
not learning instruments. It is interesting to note that it is often
these children who contribute most imaginatively to creative
tasks — perhaps because they are less inhibited about the
'correct' way of playing and because they have to listen
rather than look.

Another important aspect of supporting and motivating
young players is to provide opportunities for them to play
together in ensembles. It is here that children with differing
levels of experience and ability will listen and learn from each
other. This is also where they will develop their knowledge of
repertoire and acquire knowledge of more formal performance
practice.

You will need to educate yourself about the technical
capabilities of different instrumental beginners so that you

can find and arrange suitable music. Learning to use a music software package that will allow you to write, transpose and print music could save a lot of time. Even the most flexible published ensemble pieces may not provide you with parts for the right combination of instruments and at the right technical difficulty. Ask advice from your visiting teachers and find out what fellow coordinators in other schools use — you could exchange music sometimes.

Some schools timetable orchestra and choir sessions in lesson time, others hold them in lunchtimes or after school. There seems to be no hard and fast rule about what is best except from the music teacher's view! In a small school where a large number of children are learning instruments, lesson time might be considered more feasible. Louise has 30 minutes each for orchestra and choir on Friday mornings. Thirty per cent of the children in the school are learning and considerably more sing in the choir. The rest of her class are taught alongside another class. This causes little disruption as this class teacher and Louise team teach.

There will of course be children who give up lessons after a time and it is important that they are not made to feel failures. It would be wonderful if all children could be given the experience of learning an instrument to even a fairly modest level of attainment. There are many benefits to be gained apart from learning to play:

> ❛ Is a child who persists in violin tuition until she leaves school and then never touches a violin again a success? Is another who only takes flute lessons for two terms but then buys himself an electric guitar and forms a pop group a failure? The effectiveness of selection cannot be measured solely in terms of performing attainment or staying power. Children who end up accomplished performers are successes; but then so are those who have benefited in any other way from their lessons. These include children who have grown in confidence, or social skills, as well as those who have learnt the most modest of music skills which could act as the foundation for others in the future. (Mills, 1991: 164)

Both Louise and Rob used the word 'nightmare' to describe the whole business of organising instrumental tuition. Even where, as in Rob's school, the school secretary handles quite a lot of the administration, it seems always to be a time consuming and sometimes frenetic business. But there is a recognition that, in whatever shape or form it develops, it is a vital part of the school's music curriculum. What is needed is time for dialogue between coordinator, visiting teacher, child and parents to establish a dynamic and critical partnership which will seek to foster and integrate instrumental learning with the musical life of the whole school.

Chapter 10

Other opportunities for instrumental learning

Although commonly described as 'extra-curricular' activities, the music making that goes on outside class lessons must be viewed as an integral part of the music curriculum of the school as a whole.

What has been discussed so far is the provision of tuition by specialist peripatetic teachers for a minority of children. There will of course be many other children who want to participate in music making outside normal lesson time and where there are staff or volunteers able and willing to take this on the possibilities are great.

If you are taking up a post in a school where there has been very little or no extra-curricular music I would suggest that you should concentrate your energies on establishing activities which encourage as many children as possible to take part. Once you have generated interest and enthusiasm you might then go on to offer further opportunities.

Recorder

The most common instrument to be taught is the recorder which can suffer from being seen only as a stepping stone to 'real' instruments, or a means of teaching staff notation. The fact that large groups of children playing descant recorders can be difficult to tolerate does not help its image as a musical instrument in its own right!

There are great advantages in teaching and learning the recorder:
- it is cheap, portable, robust and relatively easy to learn in the beginning stages
- from the age of about seven (although many schools start with younger children) most children's hands are big enough to reach the holes on a descant comfortably and older children can move onto trebles and tenors quite easily
- within a few weeks children should be able to play simple tunes
- there are several good published tuition schemes available which help in structuring progression
- there is an extensive repertoire of authentic recorder music, particulary from the medieval and Renaissance/Tudor periods which may be otherwise neglected
- folk music of Europe, Asia and the Americas works well on the recorder
- a vast amount of music has also been arranged for recorders
- all the conventions of instrumental solo and ensemble playing can be established at a fairly early stage of musical development: playing with accompaniment, following a conductor, performing an independent part and following a score
- teachers with fairly limited ability can learn to play and soon take on a beginner group with your guidance

Try to avoid recorder playing becoming an isolated activity; involve recorders in class music lessons when arranging accompaniments and composing. They should blend well with classroom percussion but be aware of balance; even a small group might drown out the singers. Recorders can also be incorporated into instrumental groups alongside other woodwind etc. Introduce the treble as soon as possible to overcome the difficulties of learning the different fingering. The treble is also the instrument for which most of the original recorder music repertoire was composed.

Again there tends to be a strong gender bias towards girls with recorder playing.
- Consider positive discrimination and start a boys' group.
- Schedule lessons so that they do not always clash with the times when many children would rather be out in the playground.

■ Persuade a male teacher (if you are female) to take a recorder group.

Although there has been a tradition of schools supplying recorders it is probably more realistic to ask children to buy their own, and perhaps the tuition book also. As with any activity which involves parents having to pay, you need to consult your head and governors about the best way of handling this. If you ask children to buy a recorder you must realise that this will immediately exclude some from the activity. The question will be how big an issue it is in your particular school: if it only affects a few perhaps school funds could supply instruments, if it affects the majority then perhaps other music activities should be considered based on available resources.

Guitar and keyboard

Learning the guitar or keyboard is increasingly popular. Specialist peripatetic teachers may be available but you might find that a colleague or parent is willing to take a group. You will need to make sure that they have appropriate skills and teaching style. Although it is an advantage in cost terms you might find it difficult if things do not progress satisfactorily. This situation can also arise where you are inheriting such 'lay-teaching'. Well meaning, self-taught players can often adopt an inappropriate teaching style or lack the skill to detect technical problems which may cause difficulties later (e.g. right hand at the top on the recorder). On the other hand a folk guitarist might be a much better motivator of young children than the more demanding approach of the classical teacher.

The idea of a 'club' rather than 'lessons' might suggest a more informal and enjoyable context for learning to some children; they may feel that there is less pressure on them to make a long term commitment.

Enthusiasms within the school community can lead to all kinds of music groups: steel band, drumming, folk dancing, composing club, music technology, early music and so on. Your concern should be with making sure that

Rob has a performing arts club which takes place after school for an hour each week:

It's primarily the choir and each year we put on a show. The last one we did there were over 110 children, and we don't audition. At any one time about a third of the juniors are involved. So for the Christmas carol concert the choir will sing and the speakers will come from the club as well. We work on vocal projection and clarity. It's not seen as an elitist thing as anyone can join and children can dip in and out of it as long as they commit themselves for a term. We've done a variety of things: Joseph, Along Came Man, Blast Off which have included dance, drama, slide projections and I hope to involve a local writer in devising something.

- different children are drawn in to different activities
- the technical and musical demands reinforce (for some) and enhance (for others) classroom music
- the performance skills learned outside the classroom are used in class music lessons
- any one activity on offer can be maintained over time so that children have the opportunity to improve and gain a sense of achievement
- all such groups are included in performance events during a year: assemblies, playing to a particular class, combining with similar groups from other schools (recorder days), festivals etc.

School choir/singing group

A choir or singing group is another ubiquitous feature of primary schools. When inheriting or establishing a choir you need to consider some questions about aims and management:

When and where will you rehearse?
Lunchtime (hall out of action because of school dinners), Lesson time (whole school decision).
After school (will this exclude children?).
Quality of acoustics — some spaces may be better than others.
If sessions are short perhaps children can stand throughout.

What accompaniment will you use and who will play it?
It will be much more maneagable and successful if someone else plays the piano so that you can concentrate on directing. Try to teach and learn songs without accompaniment and add when singing is confident. Vary accompaniment: guitar, piano, keyboard, percussion, none!

If all children are singing as part of class music lessons and in assembly, what is the educational purpose of also running a choir?
Your answer to this should relate closely to your policy statement for music.

If the choir is a way of extending opportunities for those children who are interested is it necessary to audition?
In the primary school context it is very difficult to justify auditioning, especially when children's voices are developing rapidly. Interest and enthusiasm should be the only criteria for joining, and, as with other clubs and extracurricular activities, perhaps a commitment of at least a term.

How will you encourage boys to participate?
Choice of repertoire, male teacher involvement.

Will there be opportunities for performing outside school?
Look for non-competitive festivals, links with community events, combining with other schools, LEA initiatives.

A word of warning

Many music coordinators are heavily committed to extra-curricular music in their school. Despite the potential for reward and enjoyment it can sometimes seem that they have become victims of their own success. The school community comes to expect the maintenance of traditions: concerts, Christmas shows, festivals etc. Music performances for parents and governors are a way of publicising and promoting the school. There are three real dangers for the quality of curriculum music; one is that expectations constrain the development of new initiatives which might draw in other children and staff. The second is that the coordinator's energies are so focused on these activities that there is a neglect of class music concerns or support for colleagues; the third is 'burn-out'. Another possible effect is that, because of such commitments, opportunities to attend to one's own professional development may be limited. This is particularly true in secondary schools but it can be an issue in large primary schools where one might have to choose between being involved in management meetings and rehearsing the orchestra.

As a newly appointed coordinator you should resist taking on too many of these kinds of activities: prioritise and delegate where possible.

An alternative approach

If you and the school as a whole find it difficult to justify the costs of instrumental tuition for a small minority of children, you might approach this aspect of the music curriculum rather differently. You may prefer to plan for specialist input which reaches all the children at certain times in their schooling. When devising schemes of work for the school there will be particular topics or stages in skill development which might benefit from special support and enhancement. It might be that you are keen to offer a particular activity or musical style in which you are not experienced.

Certain LEA providers and independent agencies offer workshops on specific musical traditions (Gamelan, Samba, Steel Band, folk music and dance of the British Isles) or particular activities (singing days, composing projects, IT workshops, instrument making). There are many professional individuals, groups and companies who focus part of their work on educational projects (residencies, collaborative composing and performance work). Some of this work is subsidised and it may also be possible to receive financial help from your regional arts association, Arts 4 Everyone (A4E) lottery funding (see Chapter 16) or commercial sponsorship. Some projects might include other art forms (opera, dance, drama, art) and are bound to draw on other curriculum areas.

If the school agrees that the money that might have gone to subsidising instrumental tuition is earmarked for such projects you may find that the impact on the school as a whole (including the staff) is much more powerful and resonant.

The professional musician as a resource

There are now a large number of groups, companies, orchestras and individuals offering workshops, concerts and residencies to schools. Cynically, one might view this as a response to changes in the criteria for funding, but it is also a reflection of the more varied, flexible and reciprocal relationships that now exist between the professional arts world and the community. Large national opera and dance companies, and orchestras invariably employ an education officer who is responsible for generating projects, liaising with schools and sometimes acting as animateur for the work. However there will be many smaller scale and more local projects in existence.

There are many different ways in which projects are designed the list below is a sample

- A professional string quartet offer a recital to the whole school. It will include some talk to introduce the instruments and the music. Children may be invited to handle and play the instruments.
- A group offer an all day workshop to 60 children to explore local folk traditions surrounding an historical event. The children recreate the songs, music and dance with the help of specialists.
- The education unit of an opera company offer a 2-part project to explore a particular opera that is being toured. Part 1 involves a day of workshops for the Year 6 children to become familiar with the story, learn some of the music (a chorus perhaps), and devise some drama and/or composition which is derived from ideas in the opera. In Part 2 the children work with their teachers to develop the work over 2 or 3 weeks and workshop givers return to see the results. At some point in the process the children see a performance of the opera.
- A composer negotiates with the teachers in a school to work through half a term (one session per week) with all the Year 4 children on developing their composing skills relating to a particular topic or musical style. The project culminates in a concert and a recording.
- A pan-African dance group with a drummer offer a workshop in which some children will play drums and percussion to accompany other children who learn some dances.
- A local HE institution offer Gamelan workshops. Children are taught to play simple pieces and understand the way the music is put together. They then compose their own pieces back in school, to accompany a shadow puppet play.
- An orchestra commission an animateur to work with a composer to produce a large scale orchestral piece which includes sections for children's compositions. The work is generated in several schools over a fairly long period and culminates in a performance of the completed work by the orchestra and the children.

These are only a very few of the possibilities. The best projects are those in which the school is fully involved in the planning and where what is offered can be fully exploited by teachers during and afterwards. In 'Setting The Scene, The Arts and Young People' (Department of National Heritage, 1996) a variety of projects are described and although the document paints a rather rosy picture it does give information on funding and might suggest some new possibilities.

Quality and appropriateness do vary considerably so try to contact schools, who have previously booked the project, for their verdict. Find out about local or regional activity by contacting the regional arts association or the LEA music inspector. The potential for enrichment, challenge, emotional and intellectual engagement are great but we should not forget the need to evaluate this kind of resource for learning as rigorously as everything else in the curriculum.

Gemini is a professional chamber group who have been doing work in schools for many years. They have developed their education work alongside their professional performance work and as a consequence of their long experience in this field they have instituted a rigorous approach to setting up and evaluating projects in school. They work closely, wherever possible with LEA advisers or inspectors who are in a unique position to advise and identify suitable schools for particular types of work. Before any project begins there will be planning meetings attended by all those involved to discuss content, practicalities (profile of pupils, accommodation, resources, timetables) and method of evaluation. Teachers who are introduced to Gemini's working methods are also invited to identify areas of professional development that might be offered. Gemini see their input as an opportunity for learning for the teachers as well as the children.

At the end of this meeting a contract is drawn up between Gemini and the schools. This ensures that arrangements are adhered to. Teachers often forget or become immune to the conditions they work in and need to be aware of the particular needs of intensive workshopping: uninterrupted blocks of time, guaranteed spaces to work in, low background noise and disturbance, all participants being present all the time (including class teachers). This is an extract from a typical document which is produced by Gemini to set out aims and objectives:

1 monitoring
- the ensemble discusses internally as the project progresses
- after each workshop Gemini's Director and the class teacher will discuss the session
- there is usually informal discussion between Gemini and the teacher during the workshop and at break
- the director keeps a diary of activities undertaken
- pupils will keep a diary
- the class teacher will write up each workshop for publication in the pack
- tape recordings will be made of performances from every workshop
- it is likely that there will be a visit to at least one session by the music adviser

2 evaluation
- pupils will keep a diary, offer verbal and written comments after the project (including self-assessment) . . .
- class teacher will keep detailed notes, make comments and tape record performances at various stages in the project . . .
- Gemini members will discuss the project and this will be written up by the director for inclusion in the pack

There will be an evaluation session after the project attended by all those involved. Here materials will be shared, discussion will take place, a summary of learning outcomes (linked to aims and objectives . . .) and an assessment of the project made.

This might seem overly detailed but it is important that schools, as well as the musicians, are clear about their responsibilities and accountability towards the children and each other. It is easy to look upon such projects as exciting one-off experiences which, at the time, will have a dramatic and stimulating effect on the whole school community but do not have a lasting impact. First, such experiences will resonate with children for a very long time especially if teachers are prepared to exploit the project fully in follow up work. Second, there is the important element of inservice for the teachers themselves, not only in terms of fresh ideas but also the opportunity to observe their own class taking part in music led by other professionals and perhaps seeing their pupils in a new light.

Part three | Planning for music

Chapter 11
Policy

Chapter 12
Programmes of study and
schemes of work

There are different types of planning that you as the coordinator will need to be engaged in and, although it may seem more efficient to do some of it on your own, the more you involve the whole staff in the process the more successful its implementation will be. Writing the music policy for the school, developing schemes of work, units and individual lessons all require a high level of shared understanding and consensus amongst the staff. The audit and research you have carried out will guide you in how ambitious policy and planning can be: if you have a number of teachers who are very unconfident and limited in their experience of teaching music it would be foolish to propose content or teaching styles which suit you and not them.

Chapter 11   Policy

The school's policy statements for music should reflect the shared values and beliefs of staff and management. Even in drawing up this document you will find that there is an educational role for you. As has been discussed already in Parts 1 and 2, values and attitudes are shaped by personal experience and knowledge, and you are likely to need to draw your colleagues' attention to, and clarify, aspects of the music curriculum of which they may be unaware or unsure.

Many LEA curriculum support and advice services will have produced guidelines for writing policies in general as well as subject specific ones. They vary in terminolgy and detail but, of the sample I have looked at, they all include the following headings:

1 **Rationale:** What is the value and purpose of music education? How does it contribute to the development of each child? How does music contribute to the school as a community?

> From a first school:
>
> Music is one way in which we can make sense of our lives. It is a universal language spanning time, cultures and disciplines. Through music we can express, represent and communicate our ideas and perceptions. Through music we may experience that which is both beyond and greater than ourselves. Making music provides opportunities for physical, intellectual, imaginative and spiritual development.

2 *Aims:* what do you intend children to learn and develop in and through music?

This sample list is offered by Paterson and Wheway (Leicestershire, 1996)

At XYZ school we aim to:

1 promote and support curriculum music for all children as an entitlement through their classroom experiences, and follow the National Curriculum in full.

2 provide experiences and resources which promote knowledge, skills and understanding in music, in relation to both their own and others' musical traditions.

3 provide learning experiences in music which promote confidence and development of the child.

4 promote a music curriculum with relevant differentiated experiences.

5 promote progression and continuity in music through careful curriculum planning and monitoring of each child, in line with the school's policies assessment and recording.

6 promote opportunities for the child to further develop musical skills through an extended curriculum.

7 promote the continuing development of expertise and confidence in music for all/relevant members of the teaching staff.

8 recognise ways in which IT skills may be incorporated into, and developed by the music curriculum and used to enhance the musical experiences of all children.

3 *Objectives:*

Who will teach music?

How much time for music: total weekly amount and timetabling?

What will be taught (with reference to NC requirements): skills, knowledge and understanding?

What provision will be made for the extended curriculum (instrumental tuition, choir, minority interests)?

What will the policy be on funding and selecting children for tuition by visiting teachers?

Will there be a lower age limit for certain activities?

What provision will be made for inviting visiting performers and animateurs to perform or work with the children?

4 Planning:
How will we plan the teaching?
Will planning be topic led, discrete or a mixture?
Who will be responsible for the different levels of planning: schemes of work (coordinator?), units and individual lessons (class teachers?)?
How will continuity and progression be assured?

5 Resources:
Where will music teaching take place?
What resources will be provided and where will they be kept (centrally or in individual classrooms)?
Will particular teaching materials be used such as published schemes, TV or radio broadcasts?

6 Assessment, recording and reporting:
How will these be managed (by individual teachers; across each key stage)?
What methods will be used and how often will reporting be formal (consistent with other policy documents)?

7 Equal opportunities:
What provision will be made to ensure that all children have access to what is offered regardless of gender, special needs or cultural background?

8 Information technology:
How will all children be given opportunities to use IT to support their learning in music?

9 The role of the music coordinator: responsibilities

10 The role of the head teacher: responsibilities

11 Safety

12 Monitoring effectiveness of policy

13 General issues: names of staff involved in writing the document, date for review, date when policy was agreed by governing body, references.

You may have a common format for all policies in the school or you may be free to devise your own, in either case you will need to consider how best to incorporate everything you feel needs to be stated in a clear, coherent style. If the document is going to mean anything it must be accessible to all who may need or want to read it. It must also be realistic and inspiring. Teachers will often feel that they are being asked to produce documentation which is overly detailed, irrelevant or bureaucratic. However the policy document is the one place where you can publish ideals and principles. It should not be only a reflection of what is happening already, however impressive that is, but what the school aspires to.

Steps to producing a policy document

1 Read through all the existing policy documents for the school, talk to the headteacher or deputy headteacher about format and procedures.

2 If you have discovered, through the audit, that practice is patchy, attitudes and confidence are very varied amongst the staff, and music provision has been generally neglected, then you will need to attend to this before producing a policy. The staff as a whole needs to have some knowledge and understanding of what constitutes a music curriculum before making decisions about its future direction. You will need to persuade the headteacher and governors to let you work for a year with colleagues on improving classroom practice through staff workshops, demonstration or shared teaching, before embarking on this task. On the other hand, it may be more a question of revising, or updating the existing policy to reflect current practice and consider new directions. In this case it is still wise to give yourself time to appraise current provision and practice before going on to the next step. This takes us back to the audit which, apart from providing you with information and evidence of the state of music in the school, could lead directly into this process.

3 Ask for time in a staff meeting, or a meeting devoted to this one item, when you can lead the staff in a discussion about aims and objectives. The 'structured discussion' (pp. 45–47) would be appropriate here. This stage is very

important; if consultation is not full or consensus is not reached it will be very difficult to produce, let alone implement, a policy.

4 Produce a draft policy to be circulated to all staff before bringing it to a staff meeting for discussion. You might do this on your own or with the help of one or two other teachers who are confident and experienced with teaching music. If this exercise is completely new to you seek advice from the LEA, music teacher colleagues in other schools and other subject coordinators in your school.

5 Write a second draft incorporating points agreed at the meeting, and circulate again.

6 Write the final version after a second round of responses have been considered (hopefully, at another staff meeting).

7 Present to the board of governors for final approval.
  In policy documents I have looked at there is evidently a wide range of interpretations of what such documents should contain. Some limit themselves to what might be described as over-arching principles. Others look more like a teacher's handbook with outlines of the curriculum content for each year, lists of resources etc.

I would recommend that a distinction is made clearly between the policy, which should be available to parents, governors, inspectors and staff; and the music 'handbook', which is most relevant to the staff and inspectors. The policy should be included in the handbook but also should appear alongside the other policy docments for the school. Guidelines offered by Leicestershire LEA suggest the following content for a Music handbook:

Schemes of work — Policy — Staffing — Assessment — Resources — Accommodation — Development plan — Finance — Extra-curricular activity — Instrumental lessons — Continuity and liaison — IT — Equal opportunities — Sanctions and rewards

Such handbooks should be relevant and readable to all who teach music in the school, and based on current provision and practice. Several coordinators I have interviewed have made copies for every class teacher to keep in their own classroom.

Chapter 12   Programmes of study and schemes of work

Schools adopt a variety of methods to draw up plans to show what is intended that children should learn and how and what teachers will teach. The National Curriculum Orders (for England and Wales) provide a framework for assessment in presenting programmes of study and statements of attainment for the end of each Key Stage expectations. For reasons of 'simplicity', levels within each Key Stage are not given. This we should be grateful for as it offers us greater freedom to devise our own approaches and content. On the other hand, it does mean more work for the teacher, and in particular the coordinator, in drawing up schemes and units of work.

Planning must support and reflect what children are able to achieve. It may still be the case that in many schools we overestimate what teachers can competently teach and underestimate what children are capable of. As the coordinator you may find yourself rather frustrated by this and will need to accept the necessity for long term goals. Despite this, there is still a wealth of activities, opportunities and experience that can be offered to children which will be within the capabilities of all teachers if they are willing to try. You may feel the need to provide some of the expertise needed, particularly with Year 6 teaching, but this should be properly discussed and planned for.

The purpose of planning should be to provide a clear framework for all teachers and pupils by which continuity and progression can be achieved. Continuity ensures that skills and understanding can be accumulated, developed, practised and applied through a year, from one year to the next and from one school to the next. Continuity goes hand in hand with progression as the latter depends on the former: without regular engagement there is little possibility that children (or teachers) will be able to increase their understanding or skills in music. One can find the situation where music activity is going on throughout a school with little discernible progression from one year to the next, except that which can be attributed to normal development (see box).

Before we get too depressed it should be noted that these remarks were made based on findings from inspections carried out in 1993 and 1994 when the National Curriculum did not yet apply to Years 5 and 6. However, I suspect that this situation is still manifest in many schools for the simple reason that there are still many teachers who are unsure about what to teach and what to expect from children. Planning is the means by which these questions can be answered.

There are essentially three levels of planning which you will be involved with:

1   **Long-term** which offers an overview of the curriculum through all years of the school.

2   **Medium-term** which presents the learning aims and a summary of content for each term: these tend to be organised as units of work lasting, typically, four or six weeks and often coinciding with cross-curricular topics. All the teachers for a year group or even a whole Key Stage, should be involved with planning at this level. As coordinator you should also be included or at least consulted to ensure progression and continuity.

3   **Short-term** where classteachers plan the individual lessons within a unit. In the case of music it is not unusual to find coordinators providing this level of planning for colleagues. One would hope that, as a result of the support you offer, eventually all teachers will be responsible for this.

Long and medium term planning

A scheme of work is the means by which teachers translate aims and National Curriculum requirements into practice. It sets out the learning experiences and activities which children will engage with during each year of schooling. There are many approaches and models to choose from: there may be an established format already used in the school. LEA curriculum support teams have also produced guidelines and formats which might be worth investigating; be prepared to adapt frameworks to suit the particular needs of music. There is an advantage in designing your own scheme from scratch in that the process will give you confidence (and authority) when sharing it with colleagues. However, by comparing two or three existing models and making a thoughtful choice you may save yourself much time.

Planning for progression

Teachers will need to have an overview of expectations for music learning for their year. The difficulty with this is that, depending on the quality of what went before, a particular class may exceed or fail to reach the level suggested by either the National Curriculum statements or other external guidelines.

Expectations rise in two ways:
1   as a result of teachers' knowledge of how musical ability develops
2   as a result of teachers' observations through experience of what most children can achieve at a particular age or stage.

If teachers have worked in a variety of schools and with different ages they will have realised that the greatest influence on musical development is the amount of time children are involved actively with music, the quality and range of musical experiences provided and the enthusiasm with which it is taught.

If a reception class sing every day, dance and listen to music, play with musical materials and talk about their music, their music-making and their responses will become more sensitive, controlled and expressive than those of a class who listen once a week to a radio broadcast and attempt to join in with assembly singing. There is no research evidence to suggest that some children are inherently more musical than others. The differences are largely to do with the amounts of exposure to live music, encouragement, positive role models and opportunities for creative play.

The publication *Expectations in Music at Key Stages 1 and 2* (SCAA, 1997) contributes some useful guidance:

> *Some teachers have found it helpful to identify, in simple terms, what they expect all the class to achieve, what they expect most of the class to achieve, and what they expect a few of the class to achieve.*

SCAA provide recorded examples of children singing and composing to help teachers with this. What would be even more useful is for the school to collect this evidence from their own children (as is being done with other subjects) to provide a folio of exemplars for each year group.

In conjunction with such material, or without it, you might undertake this task with colleagues (see Suggestion).

It may be revealed that different year groups seem to be working at the same levels of achievement (or expectation). This in itself should generate some useful discussion and help you to identify areas for your attention. You can then take these away and devise a grid to show progression across all years. I have included an extract (Figure 12.1 p. 142) from one example.

As an initial exercise this should help colleagues see beyond their own class, but be aware of the dangers of oversimplification. Progression grids deconstruct learning in a way which is perfectly acceptable to teachers who know what the 'whole' looks (and sounds) like. However, for inexperienced teachers of music, it may lead them to dis-integrate rather than integrate the strands of the curriculum.

Suggestion

(For a whole staff INSET session) Ask teachers to imagine themselves as different children in their class.

In a circle each teacher in turn, makes a statement of what they know, understand or can do in music e.g.

'I can keep a steady beat with everyone else when listening to music'

'I know what an ostinato is, and can invent and play one if given a few notes to choose from'

'I can compose, in a group, a piece to go with a story'

'I understand that I need to watch and listen for when to start and stop playing'

As this activity is happening you should note them on a board. Then, as a group, look at the different kinds of skills, knowledge and understanding that are represented. The group should then be able to group statements under the different elements. Gradually a general profile of each year group should begin to emerge.

TEXTURE	DYNAMICS	KEY STAGE
■ Everybody makes the same sounds, sings altogether etc. ■ Play a game where the leader is making different sounds to the rest of the group ■ Introduce simple accompaniments such as a drum beat to a song ■ Play listening games to focus awareness on layers of sound e.g. Kim's games with sounds ■ A group makes more than one sound together, and at the same time to build up a texture e.g. a rainstorm with body sounds ■ Build up a composition made of different parts e.g. fireworks on bonfire night	■ Identify loud and quiet sounds in the child's environment ■ Play games to develop an understanding of loud and quiet ■ Explore loud and quiet body and vocal sounds ■ Collect loud and quiet sounds and make a sound tape e.g. a quiz ■ Using instruments to make loud and quiet sounds ■ Following hand signs, practise getting louder and quieter with voices, bodies, and instruments ■ Compose a piece to illustrate a story emphasising dynamic changes ■ Use appropriate signs and symbols relating to dynamics within a graphic score ■ Identify and respond to changes in dynamics in a piece of music e.g. through movement	Key Stage One
■ Perform/compose in layers from a graphic score ■ Add a drone as an accompaniment to a song or composition ■ Use an ostinato in a group composition ■ Sing rounds and partner songs ■ Identify when a solo instrument is playing in a concerto or piece e.g. Peter and the Wolf ■ Recognise the difference between a melody and chords ■ Experiment with clusters of notes ■ Use chords as an accompaniment to a song and in their own compositions ■ Recognise part singing in a choral piece	■ Listen to a piece of music that uses dynamics/silence for dramatic effect and use these ideas in compositions, and performance ■ Discuss where loud/quiet and silence would be appropriate in a musical piece ■ Discuss using balance of dynamics in a composition ■ Use formal signs for dynamics e.g. f, mp, p < > etc.	Key Stage Two

FIG 12.1
Progressing through the elements (source: 'A Guide to Music in Your School KS1 and 2' produced by Oxfordshire Country Music Service, Music Advisory Team)

There are two approaches to showing progression in music learning:
■ the first is based on the skills, knowledge and understanding related to recognising, exploring, selecting, controlling and manipulating musical elements of pitch, rhythm, dynamics etc.
■ the other is based on the different activities or strands described in the curriculum: singing, playing instruments, composing, improvising, recognising, responding, describing and recording.

As the coordinator you will need to help your colleagues gain understanding of progression in both, showing how they depend on each other. Without it they will continue to be highly dependent on you to provide the answer to 'what next?'. Through the INSET you are able to offer they should gradually detect progression in their *own* practice and will then be more aware of progression in their children's musical behaviour.

Here is a summary for you to consider. You will need to simplify the language and find practical examples when discussing any of this with colleagues.

What characterises progression in performing?

The ability to perform with increasing control and expression:

- longer pieces, longer phrases within a piece, slow moving melodies with sustained notes

- melodies with either chromatic movement or which leap about, or involve unusual tonal relationships.

- faster moving 'busy' rhythms, irregular or fragmented rhythm patterns, unusual or unpredictable accents.

- on an increasing range of instruments (i.e. those generally used in class music lessons).

- more complex textures

- unusual harmonies or cross-rhythms.

- greater dynamic range and greater demand for subtle changes

- sudden, dramatic changes of dynamics or speed.

- pieces in which there are subtle changes of mood or style.

- with greater responsibility on individual performers (solo; one player per part)

- with greater demand on performer to interpret music for themselves

- with greater awareness and sensitivity to others when performing with others

- with greater awareness of communicating to the audience.

What characterises progression in composing?

Increasing ability to manipulate and control musical elements (as described above) in order to interpret, communicate and express ideas or feelings.
Increasing knowledge and understanding which enables the composer to achieve a musical intention.
The ability to work, knowingly, within a particular style or convention.

'MUSIC FROM STORIES'

Performing and Composing; Compose and perform music derived from situations in a story.

Listening and Appraising; Listen to and talk about musical features within music which picture a character or scene.

The following activities represent a full programme of work to cover and extend the requirements of the Music Order. These are neither prescriptive nor exhaustive but are designed to provide a variety of starting points. It is not intended that they will be followed consecutively nor is it intended that each activity will be undertaken by every year group.

LEARNING OBJECTIVES	SUGGESTED ACTIVITIES AND WAYS OF WORKING	RESOURCES
Pupil: — sings songs; — adds accompaniments; — invents rhythm patterns; — composes simple pieces using musical elements within structures; — listens to and talks about own and other composers' music; — listens to the use of various musical instruments to create an effect; — uses knowledge gained in own compositions; — uses and responds to symbols and visual signals; — uses appropriate technology;	Warm-up activities to include those which encourage the exploration of specific musical elements, as appropriate, and the creation of dramatic atmosphere. Sing songs and when appropriate, add accompaniments, tuned and rhythmic. As and when appropriate, listen to the following pieces: (This music was often used in silent movie 'chase' scenes. See 'Stig of the Dump' Activities 1) ⟹ 'Hunt Quartet' — Mozart (See 'Stig of the Dump' Activities 1) ⟹ The Horn Concertos — Mozart (See 'Stig of the Dump' Activities 1) Composition Activities 1 — 'Stig of the Dump': There are opportunities for composition at various stages of the story: ■ The ground gives way . . . (a sudden contrast of state. Calm to chaos. Explore any single or combination of musical element.) ■ Five people meet for the first time but do not speak the same language . . . (Invent a conversation in sound but not voices — takes turns to 'speak' using the new language and then all talk at once.) — Sing 'Ging gang goolie' and/or explore 'Back Slang' and encourage pupils to invent their own. Alternatively 'scat' in a jazz style as in 'Boom shu wah'. ■ Plumbing! . . . Invent a piece of music describing the journey of Stig's water supply — mudguard — tube of the vacuum cleaner — weed-killer can — or invent your own route.) ■ Felling trees . . . Using only wooden sounds invent a piece about felling a tree, with axe, chainsaw and small hand saw. Finally, light a match and start a fire. ■ Hunting . . . Listen to the appropriate music (above) and design your own hunting call using a pitched instrument. Try to capture the essence of a signal — repeated patterns and limited number of pitch notes. ■ Meeting an enemy . . . design a music/drama/dance 'ritual' to include the giving of gifts, awaiting a response, the outcome, finish with the invention of an 'oath of secrecy of the den' using only voices. ■ Alone in a house . . . design a composition which includes the following sections; alone in a house; burglars; catch and chase (see listening above); police reward. ■ Caveman village . . . using only instruments from another culture invent 'different' music — the culture could be from your imagination and the music could be as far from convention as you like but remember that music is structured sound with an intention. Save the compositions on tape or disk and on paper, using appropriate notations. Use Music/I.T. tape recording and appropriate notation as and when desirable throughout the Key Stage.	Repertoire — Songs: 'Stig of the Dump' — Sing a Story No.5. 'Back Slang' — Sonsense Nongs, page 23. 'Ging gang goolie' — Trad. Sonsense Nongs, page 23. 'Boom shu wah' — Rip Roaring Round Book, page 92. Listening: 'Where the Wild Things Are' — Oliver Knussen. 'Alla Turca' — Mozart. 'Hunt Quartet' — Mozart. The Horn Concertos — Mozart. Any examples of Fanfares. Any examples of Silent Movie Music. Music program with midi-keyboard to play back compositions. Resources — Stories: 'Stig of the Dump' — Clive King. Orchestral Instruments where available. Specific examples refer to either the Performing Arts (Music) File 1992 or to the new Performing Arts Cornwall (Music) File 1995.

(Source: Cornwall Primary Curriculum Planning Pack: Key Stage 2 Spring/Summer C — Music for Stories Section)

FIG 12.2 **Planning through a topic or theme**

The ability to develop ideas and sustain a chosen style.
The ability to surprise, unsettle, or move the listener.

What characterises progression in listening and appraising?

All the above.
Increased ability to respond expressively and imaginatively to music.
Recognition and appreciation of an increasingly wide repertoire.
Increasing ability to express musical intentions, interpretations, responses and evaluations through appropriate language.

Progression in music is not a straightforward climb up a ladder. It is better visualised as a spiral which not only widens, but in which the line of the spiral thickens: the learner carries more and more skill, understanding and knowledge into each new musical experience.

Over the course of a year children should have opportunities to develop their skills, knowledge and understanding in music through activities which integrate composing, performing and appraising. This means that, ideally, each unit should achieve this. In practice the emphasis and focus will shift: although it is not difficult to ensure that performing will be featured much of the time, composing might be neglected and appraising limited. The whole year overview allows you to see where the 'holes' are.

Many schools still plan in the context of topics or themes which may be for an individual subject or, more typically, for several. The Cornwall Advisory Service planning pack (1996) presents schemes of work for each term based on the topics which many schools are known to use: Toys and Pastimes, Light and Colour, Victorians etc. Such topics are chosen to combine learning in different areas and the pack offers 'suggested activities and ways of working' and specific resources from which teachers can plan their lessons. Some topics have a more music-specific focus e.g. Music from Stories (Figure 12.2), Sound.

Devon Curriculum Advice provides an approach to planning with examples but without giving so much detailed content. (Figure 12.3) shows the suggested method of recording the

TERM 1

TITLE FOCUS THEME	NURSERY RHYMES/TALES: Goldilocks	
MAIN ELEMENT[S]	Dynamics	ELEMENT LEVELS Extremes loud/quiet
MAIN ACTIVITIES movement sounds with stories		SKILL LEVELS Control loud/quiet on untuned percussion —
REPERTOIRE [performing]		REPERTOIRE [listening] Carmina Burana : Orff ana
I.T.		
	Number of weeks 5	Ref.no

TITLE FOCUS THEME	NURSERY RHYMES/TALES: Hickory D.	
MAIN ELEMENT[S]	Pitch	ELEMENT LEVELS Extremes high/low movement up/down
MAIN ACTIVITIES making up/down patterns		SKILL LEVELS Explore tuned percussion —
REPERTOIRE [performing] Hickory Dickory Dock		REPERTOIRE [listening] Carnival of Animals : Kangaroo
I.T.		
	Number of weeks 3	Ref.no

TITLE FOCUS THEME	NURSERY RHYMES/TALES: Hare and Tortoise	
MAIN ELEMENT[S]	Tempo	ELEMENT LEVELS Extremes fast/slow
MAIN ACTIVITIES listening and movement		SKILL LEVELS recognising fast/slow
REPERTOIRE [performing]		REPERTOIRE [listening] Norwegian Dance 2 — Grieg
I.T.		
	Number of weeks 3	Ref.no

TERM 2

TITLE FOCUS THEME	HOUSES AND HOMES	
MAIN ELEMENT[S]	Timbre	ELEMENT LEVELS Sounds in the Environment
MAIN ACTIVITIES Making instruments Exploring through games		SKILL LEVELS
REPERTOIRE [performing] Song about houses/homes		REPERTOIRE [listening]
I.T. Recording sounds		
	Number of weeks 5	Ref.no

TITLE FOCUS THEME	USING THE WHOLE VOICE	
MAIN ELEMENT[S]		ELEMENT LEVELS
MAIN ACTIVITIES Games, songs		SKILL LEVELS Explore speaking, singing, vocal sounds
REPERTOIRE [performing] Varied (limited range)		REPERTOIRE [listening] Variety of singing styles — opera, jazz, rock, rap
I.T.		
	Number of weeks 5	Ref.no

TITLE FOCUS THEME		
MAIN ELEMENT[S]		ELEMENT LEVELS
MAIN ACTIVITIES		SKILL LEVELS
REPERTOIRE [performing]		REPERTOIRE [listening]
I.T.		
	Number of weeks	Ref.no

TERM 3

TITLE FOCUS THEME	AROUND OUR SCHOOL	
MAIN ELEMENT[S]	Duration	ELEMENT LEVELS Extremes long/short Steady beat
MAIN ACTIVITIES movement composing		SKILL LEVELS
REPERTOIRE [performing] Make up class song about our school		REPERTOIRE [listening] Anything with steady beat
I.T.		
	Number of weeks 4	Ref.no

TITLE FOCUS THEME	SUMMER CONCERT	
MAIN ELEMENT[S]	Texture	ELEMENT LEVELS Single sounds or several together
MAIN ACTIVITIES Dance and sound composition		SKILL LEVELS Presenting to audience
REPERTOIRE [performing]		REPERTOIRE [listening] African drumming — call and response
I.T.		
	Number of weeks 5	Ref.no

THE YEAR IN OUTLINE
Planning sheet 2

Year: 1

(Devon Curriculum Advice Music)

(Source: Devon Curriculum Advice — Publications)

FIG 12.3 Planning for a year

TITLE		
FOCUS *'Funeral' from 'Cry Freedom'*	*'I have a dream' from Martin Luther King's speech.*	
THEME		

MAIN ELEMENT[S]	ELEMENT LEVELS	REVIEW
Dynamics	*Introduce the 5 notes of main theme G, A♭, B♭,*	ACTUAL OUTCOMES
Pitch	*C, D♭ — Note the gradual build up of dynamics*	
MAIN ACTIVITIES	**SKILL LEVELS**	
Using 5 notes, compose short piece using voices	*Sing main phrase — in groups — build up dynamics*	
& instruments	*by introducing other group — play phrase on*	
	pitched percussion or hand chimes	
REPERTOIRE [performing]	**REPERTOIRE [listening]**	CHANGES to
Compositions based upon 5 notes	*'Funeral' from 'Cry Freedom'*	THE NEXT UNIT OF WORK — or to
Tunes around 'God bless Africa'		THIS UNIT IN THE FUTURE
I.T.	WHOLE CLASS *Singing, listening activities*	
Recording own compositions —	GROUP *Instrumental work*	
play back & listen	PAIR *Working on a tune for 'I have a dream'*	
	INDIVIDUAL	
CROSS CURRICULAR LINKS	**WHOLE CURRICULUM SKILLS**	
Language Art	*Word bank describing extract of music — moving*	
	African piece — Background to conflict — why?	

ASSESSMENT   Highlight main assessment objectives [above] and related tasks [below]

[a] Control sounds made by the voice and a range of tuned and untuned instruments	[b] Perform with others and develop awareness of audience venue and occasion	[c] Compose in response to a variety of stimuli, and explore a range of resources
Listen to vocals in piece — Introduce main tune, singing in group, gradually add other groups to build up dynamics — emphasis upon unison singing & playing — attention a control of long notes & dynamic changes	*Spoken verse — Adding 2 or 3 simple accompanying parts tuned & untuned percussion — & voices Read through creative writing — using musical accompaniment for background*	[d] Communicate musical ideas to others *5 note phrase — children to compose answering phrases Short piece using the same 5 notes called 'Our dreams' — introduce unison playing/singing — develop dynamics — repeat phrases — copy & echo — build up to a full sound — Graphic score to represent their compositions — Graphic score to evoke mood of 'Cry Freedom' As above — record compositions* using notations and recording equipment where appropriate

[f] Respond to and evaluate live performances and recorded music including their own and others' compositions and performances	[e] Listen to and develop understanding of music from different times and places, applying knowledge to their own work
— Describe how they feel about the "Funeral" music *— Develop word bank* *— Describe each group's compositions* *— Discuss creative writing & paintings in groups.* *Focus upon 5 note phrase — listen specifically for changes in dynamics & building up to climax.* Questions to be asked	*— Identify voices (chorus in unison — unaccompanied)* *— Female voices — male counterpart — repetition* *— unison again* *— Back to beginning of phrase adding string accompaniment & drum roll* *— strings higher & tambourine* *— How is the music developed?* *Does the music create a picture? How does it end?*

Year *3–5*	Class *3*

(*Source:* Devon Curriculum Advice — Publications)

FIG 12.4 A unit of work

principal content for units of work throughout a year for Year 1 children. This then translates into another stage where the detail for each unit is recorded. (Figure 12.4) shows an actual unit planned by a Year 3 teacher.

There is a danger in the cross-curricular approach of the particular needs of music becoming lost or distorted. This is why your 'specialist' overview is so important. You will be responsible for advising colleagues about how appropriate or useful it is to include music in any topic. Sometimes it might serve the interests of music better to be left out of certain topics: a song about Vikings may be musically trite and do little to support children's knowledge of Viking history, but using a Norse myth as a vehicle for a composing or dance/drama project could be very worthwhile. There is also the danger of isolating the music of particular parts of the world in this way, i.e. only including music from Japan when the topic is 'Japan'. Although it is important to celebrate uniqueness and differences, and to put music in its context, one should also be to able focus on the common musical elements which are present in all kinds of traditions and styles: drones, pentatonic scales, interlocking rhythms. From experience of working with coordinators it is clear that, as long as the format and guidelines are well-designed, realistic and reflect existing practice, teachers will be happy to adopt and adapt them to their individual way of working.

Planning a unit of work will need to include:

Year	Class	Timescale	Focus
Main learning aim/s		Activities	NC references
Management		Differentiation	Resources IT
(whole class, group etc.)			
Intended/Actual outcomes			What next

If a common format is used for planning in other subjects see if you can adapt it or consult colleagues about an alternative. Planning must be useful, enabling and flexible. It must also carry enough detail to inform or remind colleagues the following year, and for inspection purposes.

Short term planning

Learning aims for individual lessons should be focused on specific skills and particular aspects of knowledge and understanding. The planned activities are the means by which children will achieve or work towards these. Encourage teachers to identify their aims so that they are able to evaluate and assess what takes place. The aims should be focused as much on ways of working as they are on the quality of a final performance, as it is the former which will dictate the latter.

The most rewarding lessons and the most creative teaching occurs when teachers can improvise, respond to what children offer, and recognise when an unplanned event can still serve the overall learning aim. Lesson plans are not scripts and should be as much a response to what was or was not learned in the previous lesson as a projection of what will happen next.

Individual teachers will be more or less detailed in their plans: the less confident they are the more detail they will probably want. As coordinator you will need to be sensitive to the needs of each teacher and adapt your level of support accordingly. In the initial stage of encouraging a colleague to teach music you may be providing step-by-step 'recipes'; it is important to gradually wean them off this level of dependence, for both your sakes! Other, more confident teachers will just need to sound you out about their ideas.

Part four | Monitoring for quality

Chapter 13
Assessment

In various chapters of the previous Parts of this book I have discussed the importance of and methods for monitoring the nature and quality of what is going on. In Part 1 1 have described a number of ways in which the coordinator can find out what colleagues are doing with their own classes. Of course this will be reflected in how the children behave musically: their enthusiasm, confidence, responsiveness, sensitivity and fluency in all aspects of listening and making. A good understanding of what constitutes progression in music learning and therefore clear expectations of what children can achieve will provide a sound basis for both formative and summative assessments.

Assessment

> 6 *Assessment is essentially provisional, partial, tentative, explorat-*
> *ory and, inevitably, incomplete.*   (Drummond, 1994)

In *Assessing Children's Learning*, Drummond presents the
process of assessment as a 'crude' model.

FIG 13.1
The process of assessment
(*Source: Assessing Children's Learning,*
Drummond, 1993, David Fulton
Publishers)

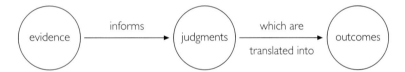

It is important to recognise that the kind of evidence a teacher
looks for, the judgments that are made and how these are acted
upon, are all coloured by the teacher's values. Discussions of
the kind suggested in Part 1 should illuminate such values and
will contribute to clarifying the nature and purpose of
assessment in music.

The most significant kinds of assessments are those made,
day-by-day, by teachers as they teach. These assessments
are formative and inform the teacher's teaching and child's
learning. In learner-teachers or experienced teachers who are
unsure about their understanding of teaching a subject, the
ability to be observant and responsive tends to be undeveloped
or suppressed. The preoccupation is with making the activity
happen, managing the resources and keeping children
engaged. As teaching skills and/or subject knowledge become

established more attention can be given to the quality of what the children are doing and evidence of their understanding.

Assessing the quality of children's music

In music, teachers have to become good listeners as well as observers. They need to recognise the different ways in which children show their musical abilities; through singing, dancing, playing instruments, inventing, describing etc. They also need to recognise the *quality* of children's work in music.

This can be done through:

- Straightforward observations during listening games, songs, rhythm work etc. Or observations made afterwards with audio or video recordings.

  Who is able to maintain a steady beat? Who is alert and responsive? Who is able to sustain long notes in a song? Who takes the lead in group work? Who shows sensitive listening through how they play or sing in an ensemble? Who often goes to the music corner to play alone?

- Questioning.

  In composing: *Tell me about your piece? What made you choose those sounds? Who thought of repeating that idea? What would you like to do with your music next?*

  In performing: *what kind of mood does this song suggest? How can we capture that mood in the way we sing? How can we make the accompaniment more interesting? What kind of introduction should we have? How can we make the sound build up?*

  In appraising: *how did that make you feel? What happened in the middle? Could you hear one instrument playing all the way through? At what kind of event might you hear this music?*

- Writing, poetry, art work, dance, talk.

  The quality of language: evidence of understanding of musical elements and structures.

Appropriate responses to repetition, contrast, dynamics, tempo etc.

Imaginative/expressive responses to music through physical gestures, patterns and forms, and through visual art.

■ Composing.

Do they put into practice musical ideas worked on as a class (ostinato accompaniments, getting quieter, canon etc)? How much musical detail do they record on their graphic score? Do they appraise their work in progress and change or refine things?

Do they take risks i.e. break the 'rules' you have given them.

■ Self evaluations: music diary, simple questionnaire, or some form of 'record of achievement'

What did you enjoy most about that project/task? What did you find easy/difficult? What are you now able to do in music that you couldn't do before? I can . . . I found out that . . . I liked . . . I need to try . . . again.

Using a tape recorder should become second nature for teachers in music lessons. It allows you to record individual responses (however brief), composing in process and finished performances. Such records will help in formative assessments and, when necessary, writing reports. Children may also be able to use them to appraise their own progress and make copies of work they feel proud of.

Alongside taped records you will also need to keep written records on the progress of each child. From my experience of talking to teachers it appears that keeping records on children's learning in music as well as some other foundation subjects, is still rather minimal. There needs to be a compromise between the need to recognise and value children's achievements in music, and avoiding meaningless box-ticking.

A lot of musical activity engages children in unison performing (whole class singing) or ensemble work (group composing and performing) where it is difficult to identify individual achievement. In fact, the need to do this may well lead to some change in the balance of activities. Alongside the identification of what is to be assessed in a unit of work, it will be helpful to note how the evidence will be gathered: through observations of a particular group's approach to a composing task, through listening to some individual improvisations in a circle game, through recording a singing-the-register session, through conversations with children about their composition. Some assessments can be made 'on the hoof' others need time. It is not sensible or feasible to attempt to assess every child in any one lesson but over a unit of four or five weeks it should be possible to comment on the achievements of most if not all the children. You might decide to devise a method which only needs you to note exceptions to achievement i.e. record those who exceeded expectations and those who are still 'working towards'.

When reporting formally remember to keep the language simple and meaningful: using the language of National Curriculum documents may be alienating to parents. Some reports I have seen give a summary of the work covered during the term or year, informing parents about the kinds of musical activities undertaken. This is followed by a fairly brief report on the child's achievements. Of course, one of the best ways of letting parents know how their child is doing in music is for them to hear them composing and performing, live. Assemblies, small scale performance as well as whole school events should show parents a broad picture of curriculum music and their child's engagement with it.

Direct experience will also be a better way of informing the music teachers at KS3 about what children in your school can do in music. Invite the music teachers from the secondary schools to which most children progress, to attend performance events or send them tape recordings of Year 6 work. Better still, involve them in a summer term project aimed at Year 6 and Year 7.

The professional dialogue and collaborations that you generate with other music teachers will greatly benefit everyone involved: children, teachers and the community as a whole. You will find yourself part of a support network, rather than isolated, and contributing to one stage in the musical journey which children make throughout the whole of their life in school.

Part five Resources for learning

In this part I have attempted to gather together information and suggestions related to a variety of resources. Printed materials, instruments, equipment, human expertise are all included, as well as some thoughts on how one might enhance the learning environment. I have also included a chapter on copyright and royalties which will, hopefully, clarify the legal restrictions on copying and performing published music in school.

Chapter 14

Music corners and music work stations

In most nurseries and infant classrooms, and in some junior classrooms, it is common to see tables, or an area of the room, set up with a variety of materials or apparatus. These areas are designed to offer children opportunities to learn through exploring, manipulating, experimenting, i.e. independent research and practise.

Sand, water, the home corner, a table of yellow objects, autumn leaves and seed pods, Lego, etc. can all be found at one time or another. What is less common is a sound or music corner. This is a pity as it can be a source of much support and extension to children's learning in music. With technology it is also more possible to carry this idea right through the junior age range. Children, alone or with a partner, can make discoveries and pursue their own ideas. You may find through the audit that the KS1 teachers already have sound or music corners in their classrooms and consequently it should be fairly straightforward to develop the connections between this and whole class music activity.

Activities might be quite specific or very open, here are some examples:
- Try different beaters on different instruments and discover how the sound changes.
- How many scraping sounds are there? Can you make patterns of long and short sounds?

- Practise tapping some rhythm patterns (from names of animals drawn on cards) on the slit drum.
- On the computer compose some music using rhythm layers.
- Have a musical conversation with a friend on 2 xylophones.
- Several different sized earthenware flower pots are suspended from a washing line — how does the pitch change? Can you invent a tune for flower pots?
- Invent sound patterns to interpret some graphic notation drawn onto flashcards.
- Invent music to accompany a sequence of pictures which tell a story.
- Using a CD-ROM package find out how brass instruments have changed since medieval times.
- Make up a tune to go with a rhyme using these chime bars.
- Improvise a melody over a single finger chord pattern played by a partner on the keyboard.
- With a partner, invent some music to accompany the story you have written. Use a tape recorder to record it.

Whatever is offered needs, in some way, to connect with the music learning that is planned for the whole class. Such activities should extend and support what happens in lessons and you will need to make sure you can monitor and evaluate how it is used (which children habitually use it, and which never use it?). If children have composed a piece or discovered something, time should be found for this to be shared with the rest of the class. It may stimulate further work for a music lesson.

A music listening corner should also be considered. This would consist of a tape recorder and headphones (perhaps two or three sets with a splitter box). Children can then listen again to music heard in a lesson, listen to music they choose from a selection, or carry out a listening task directly linked to planned work.

The music corner can be used for children to display their work: home-made sound makers, found sounds, graphic scores, art work or writing stimulated by music.

There is, of course, the problem of noise and space and both these need to be dealt with sensitively. It may not be sensible to have it set up throughout the week, but available at specific times.

These are some suggestions that arise from what I have seen in classrooms:

- use a box, bag, suitcase or something like a shoe tidy; these can be put away and brought out at chosen times
- locate the activities in a play tent (dome type) or play house. This cuts down the noise and helps focus attention, especially for listening
- a book display unit or screen strategically placed can cut down noise levels
- check health and safety particularly regarding volume levels on tape recorders, and electric cables
- institute some guidelines for how many children can use it at any one time, and for care of the materials and equipment

Never allow the corner to become too cluttered, or to become a 'crash, bang, wallop' corner, and do not feel obliged to make it a permanent feature of the classroom. If you have little experience of including this idea in your classroom, make sure you try it out yourself before advocating it to your colleagues. It will not suit every teacher or every classroom but used judiciously it should

- increase the amount of contact children have with music,
- support learning aims,
- allow children to consolidate and extend their skills and knowledge,
- encourage individual creativity.

Chapter 15

Resource management

Music is a practical subject using a wide variety of resources and, as the coordinator, you need to be well-informed and well-organised. Timetabling and accommodation, in particular, can have a significant effect on the quality and range of what goes on. Each of these topics should be addressed as part of your audit and subsequent reviews. Where appropriate you should include statements in the policy document and some kind of checklist in your 'music folder' as a reminder.

Health and safety in music

When music in school consisted mainly of singing, one might imagine that there were few risks involved for children and teachers; apart from falling off makeshift stages or fingers trapped in music stands. With increased diversity in music making which involves instruments and electronic equipment, subject coordinators need to be more aware of possible health and safety issues.

There are two main contexts which present risks with potentially serious consequences:
1 electrical equipment: keyboards, tape recorders, computers, hi-fi systems
2 handling and storing instruments: percussion, pianos, orchestral instruments etc.

The risks in primary schools are often more evident and acute for several reasons. Music is often taught by teachers who have not had specialist music training and are therefore less aware of possible dangers. They are also less used to handling musical instruments and may be less aware of their construction, movable parts, weight etc. If teachers are not sure about how to manage the equipment in their teaching there are more likely to be accidents to both humans and instruments! Anxiety or excitement makes people careless. Teachers and children need to adopt good routines and habits around music equipment of all kinds.

Electrical equipment
- Check leads and plugs regularly and include visual checks on instruments children bring in.
- Where there is a dedicated music room and keyboards are used, consider installing circuit breakers.
- Position equipment so that cables are not stretched, trapped, wrapped round chair legs or trailing.
- Keep cables away from radiators and hot pipes.
- Do not use multi-socket adaptors.
- Do not allow liquid in the vicinity of any equipment.
- As soon as a fault or damage is detected take the equipment out of use.
- Mains adaptors get quite hot when switched on for long periods, so make sure all are switched off and disconnected at the end of a session.

Instruments
- Percussion instruments often develop splinters, chips and protruding pins. Take them out of circulation and repair or discard.
- Some cylinder shakers may have metal shot inside so check that ends are secure.
- Store large, heavy instruments such as the bass xylophone at floor level and always carry them between two people. Smaller children should not lift or move large, heavy equipment.
- Provide adequate storage for instruments so that items are not stacked on top of each other or awkward to access.
- Children should not be permitted to play recorders while moving about, especially in the playground.
- Never attempt to move a piano single handed. Upright pianos are top heavy and quite unstable.

■ A grand piano should have the legs braced. If a piano needs to be moved from one floor level to another specialist piano movers should be used.

Less serious risks involve hygiene related to playing instruments, and exposure to loud sounds. Mouthpieces of recorders and brass instruments can be soaked using sterilising solution. Whistles, panpipes or ocarinas should be made of plastic if they are to be used as classroom instruments. They can be cleaned in the same way. Wooden mouthpieces should be wiped with soaked swabs.

Fortunately the design of music stands has improved in recent years. Fold-up stands need careful treatment to avoid trapped fingers, and metal stacking stands often develop unpleasant sharp corners. If you are purchasing stands do some market research first; find out what other schools have.

In primary schools the problem of excessive noise causing damage to hearing is far less likely than in secondary schools where amplifiers are used. However be mindful that children who suffer from repeated ear infections (glue-ear) or some hearing impairment may be particularly susceptible to loud sounds of particular pitches (a wood-block played with a wooden beater, a cymbal crash). Children's sensitivity to sound is much greater than most adults'.

Check that volume levels on tape recorders and keyboards are controlled when headphones are used. Stick tape across the slider or highlight the maximum level on a dial. If you make tape recordings of listening material try to use equipment where you can set a low recording level.

Apart from the importance of avoiding accidents and ill health these measures will also preserve your musical equipment from damage and deterioration.

[Some of the information and advice offered in this section is drawn from *Health and Safety in Music Curriculum Activities* (Devon County Council).]

Accommodation: for people and equipment

 The accommodation in many primary schools is not conducive to music making: sounds made in one teaching area impinge on quiet work in another, and school halls are often too resonant.

(OFSTED, 1995)

Many schools are not in a position to provide a dedicated space for music although it would be wrong to suggest that a music room is an impossible dream. Many schools do manage to create a music room out of quite unpromising spaces and schools built in the past decade or so should have included some kind of music or drama studio. The problem is that without the attention of a coordinator such rooms can be gradually taken over by other activities and uses: storing resources, TV viewing, special needs, becoming increasingly cluttered and timetabled for other things. There is also the problem of schools with expanding rolls who need to create new classrooms from existing accommodation.

Some kinds of music activity can be accommodated quite well in the classroom if the space is flexible enough to move furniture out of the way and make room for children to sit in a circle. A lesson which is focused on listening and recording responses or ideas on paper may need no change to the room if the classroom can provide a quiet, undisturbed environment. This can be difficult to achieve in an open plan school and teachers find that they have to plan their lessons to coincide with another class going out for PE, for instance.

One of your tasks as coordinator should be to campaign for the best possible conditions in which children and their teachers can engage with music. MANA's *Notes for Governors* (1966) lists the following as desirable:

- a music studio or dedicated space for music where noise will not disturb others
- the hall
- quiet rooms for children to work in groups or at a music corner
- good storage systems in a base accessible to all classes

Apart from the accommodation needed for whole class music lessons you will also need to consider what is needed for visiting instrumental teachers and extra curricular activities.

Helen described how, during one year a spare classroom became the music room and almost immediately musical activity increased.

'much more music has happened this year throughout the school because it's so much easier to take your class to a room where all the equipment is stored and you don't have to spend ages moving furniture and equipment about. But it's only been for two terms because the new infants will start next term and it will become their classroom. So it'll be back to fetching and carrying and I expect teachers won't be so enthusiastic.'

Julie, at a middle school, gradually found that the music room was taken over by special needs work. She felt the loss of this facility affected the way she planned for music.

'I'd be there to welcome the class and the environment was already musical... we were doing some medieval dances and I was able to set everything up beforehand with a space for the dancers and a musicians' corner. But now when I work in another classroom all the tables have to be cleared, the instruments fetched and you lose the impact, it makes a big difference.'

Clare, in her first post, sees the creation of a music room as a priority in raising the status of a neglected area and improving the musical environment.

'the classrooms are so tiny and the classes are so big there is no way that you can do a proper music lesson in them. There is a 'music room' which is a tiny room which has a piano and desks in it; SEN work goes on there, extra Maths groups, English go in there, Science equipment is kept there and a few instruments as well. So I've got plans to take over another space...'

When you carry out your audit try to assess how space in the school as a whole is used as well as the space in each classroom.

- Is there a room that is dedicated to a subject or activity that does not actually use it very much?
- Are there spaces around the school that could be used for occasional group composition work without disturbing others?
- What adaptations could be made to provide better sound proofing or more flexible space? Sometimes teachers can become 'locked' into seeing the layout of their classroom in only one way. It might only take a fresh eye to identify some ways to improve things (reorganising storage, repositioning the teacher's desk/table).
- Do teachers include a sound or music corner where children can work individually or in pairs?
- Is there space for computer workstations to include a midi keyboard?
- Find out about sound absorbing materials which could be used when rooms are being refurbished: curtaining, acoustic tiles, felt or hessian covered display board, carpet (even a piece will make a difference).

If you are fortunate enough to be working in a school which is being rebuilt or extended you may have a wonderful opportunity to influence decisions and acquire some purpose built accommodation for music.

The other issue of accommodation is concerned with the storage of instruments. Instruments for curriculum music need to be well maintained, clearly identified (to help your less knowledgeable colleagues and the children), and accessible. There are various designs of music trolley and storage boxes or crates; whatever you use devise a system of labelling so that everyone knows where different items are meant to live.

If instruments need to be carried or moved around a lot on one level then trolleys may be the best answer for most items. If resources need to be taken up or down stairs then crates with handles are a good idea. Beaters can be kept in large catering tins, tubs or small plastic buckets. I have also seen wall-mounted storage for beaters and small instruments using hooks, brackets, racks or fabric pockets (like shoe tidies). Always keep a secret store of beaters to replace ones in use, and remember to buy a few pairs each year to replenish stocks.

Everyone will need to be trained to keep things in their place. The quickest way for instruments to be damaged or lost is careless treatment and storage. You will need to have secure storage for audio equipment, keyboards, CDs and tapes. If resources are well-looked after, accessible and relatively easy to move around the school, teachers are much more likely to use them in their music lessons. Instruments need to be treated with respect not treated like toys or sound junk.

Poor accommodation is debilitating and depressing.

Timetabling

For England and Wales the Dearing Review of the National Curriculum advises schools on the amount of time that children at KS1 and KS2 should have for music. This is best interpreted as one hour per week for KS1 and one hour fifteen minutes for KS2.

- Does singing in assembly count as part of the music curriculum?
- Does whole-school singing practise contribute to curriculum time?
- If rehearsals for the Christmas show, which involves lots of music performing, are in school time can these take the place of music lessons?
- Does lots of music in one term means we don't need to do any the following term?

As coordinator you will have to ensure that music is timetabled alongside all other subjects, that it cannot fall off the end of Friday because the class had 'catching-up' to do, and that KS1 teachers recognise the importance of engaging in music little and often, ideally every day (action songs, tidying up songs, singing the register, circle games, music corner) with a longer 20–30 minute session each week to develop composing and instrumental work.

With KS2, lesson lengths will need to vary according to the nature of the activities: composing needs more generous amounts of time than focused listening and performing. Avoid locking inexperienced teachers into long lessons. 40–50 minutes should be long enough for most whole class sessions with time for some focused group work, but there is no harm in reducing the time if the activity is focused on skill development or introducing new material to be developed over time. Assimilating musical skills and understanding seems to benefit from regular intense but fairly short episodes of attention.

Chapter 16   Copyright and royalties

Teachers of music in school need to be aware and take note of legal constraints on copying published music. Most teachers will know about the restrictions on photocopying written text but are less clear about the much tighter controls that exist where printed music is concerned. I have attempted to focus on the aspects of copyright law which relate to what might normally concern primary school music activity. The source for this information is the Code of Fair Practice (Music Publishers Assoc. Ltd., 1992).

Broadly speaking, all music that has been published in the past 70 years is subject to copyright. This relates to the work of composers, lyricists, arrangers, and editors. For the publishers themselves the period is 25 years; this is called the 'typographical phase'.

Photocopying, storing on a computer disk, handwriting words or music onto an overhead projector, board, or sheet of paper, or handwriting copies, are all included in the legislation. There are, however, a few exceptions within the law which should be of value.

In the classroom

■ Teachers and students are permitted to **copy by hand** in the course of instruction

- The performance of a musical work before an audience consisting of teachers and pupils . . . and others directly connected with the activities of the school (but not parents) is permitted
- In any **one quarter of a year 1% of a published musical work** may be photocopied and subsequently destroyed

An organisation called Christian Copyright Licensing offers a license to schools and churches. This covers the copyright for any songs which are included in their list of 120,000 hymns and 'worship' songs. The licence covers OHPs, service sheets and songbooks, although the words must be typed or written out rather than photocopied directly from the source. You are also covered for making a limited number of tape recordings. This might make life easier for assemblies and certain religious festivals.

Performance activity (instrumental teaching, examinations, concerts, musical productions, assemblies):

> *Copying in relation to a literary, dramatic, musical or artistic work means reproducing the work in any material form (ibid).*

For choirs, orchestras and ensembles all parts used must be purchased copies. This includes transcriptions or arrangements of a work subject to copyright. There are certain circumstances in which copies may be made but if in any doubt you should contact the particular publisher or the Music Publishers' Association.

Emergencies

Copies may be made:
- when music has been lost or damaged and it is too late to replace before a prearranged concert. A replacement must be purchased as soon as possible afterwards and the copy should destroyed. If the work is on hire the copy should be returned with the rest of the music
- for ease of performance (awkward turn)
- where a 'classroom' set of parts cannot be purchased separately then extra copies can be made for up to a 'quarter set' more

- if the music is out of print copies can be made with permission from the publisher to whom a fee may be payable

> *Illegal copying discourages creativity and investment by music publishers (ibid).*

Public performances

If you intend to perform music in a show or concert to a **paying** audience made up of parents and friends, you will need to find out whether a royalty should be paid to the publisher or to the Performing Rights Society (PRS). In the UK all musical works are automatically copyright protected once they are written down or recorded in any way. This means that, in theory, a fee could be payable on all the music you have chosen unless you or the children have composed it!

In practice things are not quite so inflexible. Most publishers who produce the kind of material used by schools will look at each enquiry or request individually. If a school were putting on a performance for purely commercial gain then a fee would be expected. On the other hand, a small school that needs to charge to cover costs could expect less strict application of the rules.

If in doubt you should contact the Music Publishers Association or the Performing Rights Society.

Chapter 17 Budgeting

One of the first things you will need to find out, when first appointed, is how the school finances are organised.

- How and when are decisions made about the budget for each subject?
- Are you invited to bid for what you want?
- To what extent does the development plan control decisions?
- How are decisions made about inservice?

However decisions are finally made you will need to become skilled at lobbying and campaigning for music. Schools are, more and more, having to plan a long way ahead and as a consequence there is not much flexibility in the system. This planning will take the form of a school development plan (SDP) which will encompass all facets of the school's operations: curriculum development and the consequent staffing and resource implications, as well as plans for improvement, innovation, expansion of provision in terms of the physical as well as the educational environment. Costs, timescale, monitoring and evaluation will all be recorded. Such development plans will break down into short, medium and long term aims, with the assumption that plans will be reviewed and revised annually.

This approach to planning has advantages and disadvantages for you as the music coordinator:

- music is earmarked for attention — but 3 years hence. In the meantime you will have to make do with a minimal budget
- your appointment has been made as a result of decisions made through the SDP, and you are able to purchase a lot of resources during your first year
- music is seen as low priority and as a result of other demands it is de-prioritised
- if planning decisions are known and agreed by all there is a high degree of accountability. Such plans should act as enablers rather than obstructors to development

Educating the decision-makers

Governors and headteachers will sometimes need to be persuaded that, although a new piano seems to be a prestigious acquisition for the school, what is really needed is a better range of percussion instruments and teaching materials, with supply time for you to work with colleagues in their classrooms. A lot of curriculum music is unglamorous and cannot be put on show, but without investment in resources and professional development the quality of teaching and learning will not improve. What money is spent on will reflect, sharply and precisely, the values and priorities which are held by the decision-makers. It is your responsibility to educate, inform and, if need be, put pressure on the management:

- suggest that one governor is given special responsibility for the arts curriculum
- take the opportunity to explain to the audience the context for composition work presented at school concerts
- find opportunities to involve the school with other schools or professional groups in collaborative projects which arise from class work. Make sure governors and parents know what is happening; create an opportunity for the outcomes of the project to be shared
- involve the local press and radio stations
- when putting forward a request for funding take care in the writing and presentation. Include a rationale: how this item or initiative will contribute to existing provision, how, if it is a project, you will evaluate its success
- invite governors to observe or join in music sessions

- hold a music workshop for parents, at an open evening, to show them what curriculum music is
- involve parents in performance events and/or music-making groups after school

Spending requirements

Although Music does not 'consume' resources quite in the way that art does there will be certain aspects of the music curriculum which will need recurrent funding: most significantly, instrumental tuition if the school has agreed to subsidise fees (see pp. 107–9). There are also relatively small amounts of money needed to keep things running, e.g.

- repairs to instruments
- piano tuning
- blank audio tapes
- replacing beaters

There will also be the need to upgrade, extend and improve resources:

- sheet music, songbooks and teachers' books
- more percussion instruments
- recorded music, software, videos
- support materials for schools' broadcasts
- posters, reference material for the library

More expensive items will probably need to be bid for especially and should be identified on the development plan:

- audio equipment
- midi keyboard
- bass xylophone
- drumkit
- published teaching scheme
- creating or refurbishing accommodation for music

Apart from what appears on the development plan keep your own list of needs and wants, reviewing priorities regularly, and remember that if you are considering the purchase of new resources you may need to consider time for INSET with colleagues to ensure that they know how to use them.

You should also include funding for projects involving professional musicians.

Consider what can be offset by fundraising or parental contributions.

Staff development

Requests for non-contact time will also need to be planned and bid for:

■ supply time for consultancy
■ supply time for auditing, monitoring and reviewing
■ courses and conferences
■ admininistration time (e.g. at the beginning of the school year to sort out instrumental tuition)

Through my discussions with teachers it is very difficult to present a typical picture or a model of good practice. However teachers in schools where proper consultation takes place, where management is open about the criteria for decision making, and where problems are tackled creatively, imaginatively, and collaboratively, are likely to feel valued and supported.

 Almost nothing of any real worth that is going to affect the important work which goes on in school, that of educating children, can take place without the support of staff.

(Amesbury in Davies and Ellison, 1994)

Other sources of funding

Lottery money

There are two routes to funding offered by the Lottery:

1 A bid for capital funds to adapt, improve, extend or build accommodation for musical activity: this might be a performance space, recording facilities or practise studios. The assumption is made that this will be for community as well as school use. Bids for equipment are also accepted e.g. instruments for a brass band, recording equipment.

The Voluntary Arts Network has produced a series of booklets entitled *Lottery Arts Capital Funding*. Two are very pertinent to music provision *Educational Establishments* and *Musical Instruments*. They set out the principles which apply to arts funding from the Lottery arts fund and offer detailed information on putting together an application that is likely to succeed,

> There has been a rush of educational establishments applying to the Lottery but their success rate has been low compared with other kinds of application. The Arts Council are not allowed to use Lottery funds for education costs already covered by local and central government and have turned down applications where, for example, the level of use by the community . . . is low, the relationship between educational and community use poorly thought out, or the scheme is a transparent piece of window-dressing for a set of educational facilities.

Seek as much help and advice as you can through your regional arts board and directly from the Arts Council if necessary.

2 Arts 4 Everyone (in England) is a new initiative, launched in 1997 by the Arts Council with Lottery money, to encourage 'new creative projects'. The aims are to

- encourage new audiences to experience high-quality arts activity
- encourage and develop participation in arts activity
- get more young people actively involved in arts and cultural activities
- support new work and help it develop its audience
- build people's creative potential through training or professional development

Grants range from £500 to £500,000 (applications for over £100,000 have to meet more rigorous criteria) and the applicants must commit at least 10 per cent of the costs (15 per cent over £100,000).

In Scotland 'New Directions' is the title given to a similar initiative focusing on arts activity rather than capital projects. One or more of these three aims have to be fulfilled

- New work
- Access and participation
- Talent, skills and creative abilities (particularly among young people).

Other sources of funding might be closer to home although not necessarily dealing with such large sums. Find out about local charities and trusts who sponsor the arts and education. Parents and governors should be a good source of information about local activity. Although it is common practice one should be careful of overexploiting the generosity of parents and friends of the school. It is dangerous to become too reliant on fundraising and donations so try to plan for long-term development.

Chapter 18

Resources for teaching

A selected range of resources are listed here, the majority of which are relatively new. I make no excuses for including some quite 'elderly' publications which I consider to be relevant and valuable. I have tried to list some specialist sources, assuming that teachers will have access to the major educational mail-order suppliers.

Recommending songs, pieces of music for listening and teaching materials is always difficult as we tend to develop our own particular taste and bias, not only in music itself but also in the style of presentation. This is why I, as a specialist, tend to favour a range of published materials from which ideas can be chosen rather than one major scheme. Less confident colleagues may find that the support of a well-designed scheme makes the difference between doing something rather than nothing!

Teaching materials

Nursery to 7 (* denotes accompanying cassette or CD)

Barrs, K. (1995) *Music Works*, Belair

Birkenshaw, L. (1982) *Music For Fun, Music For Learning*, Holt, Rinehart and Winston

Buchanan, K. and Chadwick, S. (1996) *Music Connections*, Cramer Music*

Davies, L. (1993) *Take Note* BBC*

Farmer, B. (ed.) (1982) *Springboard: Music*, Nelson

Holdstock, J. and Richards, C. (1995) *Sounds Topical KS1*, OUP*

Holdstock, J. (1984) *Earwiggo* (5 vols) available from Lovely Music, Tadcaster

MacGregor H. (1995) *Listening to Music Elements, 5+*, A&C Black*

MacKenzie, L. (1994) *Responses to Music*, Bright Ideas Series, Scholastic

Nicholls, S. (1992) *Bobby Shaftoe Clap Your Hands*, A&C Black

Orff-Schulwerk American Edition (1977–82) *Music for Children* (vols 1,2) Schott

Richards, C. (1995) *Listen to This KS1* Saydisc*

Thompson, D. and Baxter K. (1978) *Pompaleerie Jig*, Arnold-Wheaton

Umansky, K. (1994) *Three Singing Pigs*, A&C Black

York, M. (1988) *Gently Into Music*, Longmans*

7+

All the above

Adams, P. (1997) *Sounds Musical*, Oxford University Press*

Hanke, M. and Leedham, J. (1996) *Alligator Raggedy-Mouth*, A&C Black

McNicol, R. (1992) *Sound Inventions*, CUP (video available)

Richards, C. (1995) *Listen To This, KS2*, Saydisc*

9+

All the above

Burnett, M. (1993) *Music of the Caribbean* WOMAD/Heinemann*

Farrell, G. (1994) *Music of India* WOMAD/Heinemann*

Jones, G. (1994) *Music of Indonesia* WOMAD/Heinemann*

Wiggins, G. (1993) *Music of West Africa* WOMAD/Heinemann*

McNichol, R. (1996) *Music Explorer* (video and book) LSO, Discovery Dept*

Music File (1989) Mary Glasgow and now Stanley Thornes*

Orff-Schulwerk American Edition (1977–82) Music for Children (vols 2,3) Schott

Schemes

The decision to purchase a complete published scheme must be made in consultation with the staff as a whole. They tend to be quite expensive so there needs to be some careful consideration of how such a scheme will contribute to and develop practice. A scheme will not improve things on its own. Your responsibility will be to ensure that colleagues understand the particular approach offered and the importance of learning to adapt the content to suit the particular needs of a class. A scheme which accords closely with the style and approach of you and your colleagues should make life a lot easier, but, however good it is, it will not remove the need for teachers to work at strengthening their own knowledge and understanding. A certain amount of INSET will be necessary to introduce the materials to the school and you should expect to continue to mediate between the resource and the teachers. You might find that particular volumes in a scheme work are better than others and, given that they all follow a similar framework (i.e. the National Curriculum), it should be possible to be quite selective.

Edwards, M. and Fletcher, L. (1995) *Nelson Music*, Nelson*
Hart, W. (1995) *Lively Music*, Heinemann*
Silver Burdett Music (1990) (3 vols) Simon and Schuster*
Odam, G., Arnold, J. and Ley, A. (1996) *Sounds of Music*,
    Stanley Thornes*

Radio and television schools programmes

Similar considerations should be made in the use of broadcast music programmes. Many teachers have become quite dependent on this resource to the point of allowing all the content of their music lessons to be based on a particular series. In the worst scenario, the programmes replace the teacher entirely. Spend some time viewing and listening to programmes with the teachers' notes and look for ways to 'slot' them into the yearly plans. Encourage teachers to become familiar with the material before using it in the classroom; be selective with the programme content, and use the pause button.

It might be useful to use extracts from such programmes in the context of staff development.

TV/Video

Instrument Tales KS2 BBC
Music Makers KS2 BBC
Music Workshop KS2 BBC
Music Performance Packs BBC

Radio

The Song Tree KS1 BBC
Time and Tune KS2 BBC
Music Workshop KS2 BBC
The Music Machine: Making Musical Connections (1997) BBC
    (subject knowledge for teachers)
Masterclass Classic FM (subject knowledge for teachers)

Song books

(* a cassette available or included)

Allen P. (1997) *Singing Matters*, Heinemann*
Birkenshaw-Fleming, L. (1990) *Come On Everybody, Let's Sing*,
    Thompson
Connolly, Y., Cameron, G. and Singham, S. (1981) *Mango
    Spice*, A&C Black
Corp, R. (1993) *Folksongs of the British Isles*, Faber Music
Corp, R. (1993) *Spirituals from the Deep South*, Faber Music
East, H. (ed.) (1989) *Singing Sack*, A&C Black*
Floyd M. (1993) *Folksongs from Africa*, Faber Music
Gadsby, D. and Harrop, B. (1982) *Flying Around*, A&C Black
Gritton, P. (1993) *Folksongs from India*, Faber Music
Gritton, P. (1993) *Folksongs from Ireland*, Faber Music
Holdstock, J. (1996) *Doobeedy Doo, Four Concert Rounds For
    Juniors*, distributed by Lovely Music
Kempton, C. and Atkin, A. (1995) *Rip Roaring Rounds*,
    Southgate
Marsh, L. (1988) *Spooky Songs*, Piper Publications
Marsh, L. (1991) *The Toy Box*, Piper Publications
McMoreland, A. (1981) *The Funny Family*, Ward Lock*

Rosen, M. (1992) *Sonsense Nongs*, A&C Black

Sanderson, A. (1995) *Banana Splits — ways into part-singing.* A&C Black*

Sing For Pleasure Song Books from: Lynda Parker, 25, Fryerning Lane, Ingatestone, Essex CM4 ODD. Tel. 01277 353691

Singing Together, Christmas Collection, BBC

Thompson, D. and Winfield, S. (1991) *Junkanoo*, Longman*

Thompson, D. and Winfield, S. (1991) *Whoopsy Diddledy Dandy Dee*, Longman*

Tillman, L. (1991) *Mrs Macaroni*, Macmillan

Assembly song books

Brand, J. (1991) *The Green Umbrella*

Come And Praise, BBC

Fourteen Hymns and Songs for Junior Recorder Groups or Mixed Ensembles, A&C Black Tillman, J. (199?) *Light the Candle*, CUP

Topic-based and cross-curricular

Singing Together, Seasons, BBC

Astles, P. and J. (1990) *Bartholomew Fair*, OUP

Astles, P. and J. *Pilgrimage*, OUP

Bagenal, A. and M. (1987) *Music From The Past* (4 vols) Longman*

Clarke, V. (1990) *Music Through Topics*, CUP

East, H. (1991) *Look Lively, Rest Easy*, A&C Black*

Gilbert, J. (1986) *Festivals*, OUP*

Gilbert, J. (1990) *Story Song and Dance*, CUP

Marsh, L. (1990) *Footprints*, Piper Publications

Musicals

Music Performance Packs, BBC

Campbell, D. (1990) *The Bumblesnouts Save The World*, Novello

Campbell, D. (1991) *The Emerald Crown*, Novello

Rose, P. and Conlon, R. (1987) *African Jigsaw*, Weinberger

Rose, P. and Conlon, R. (1991) *Ocean World*, Weinberger

Rose, P. and Conlon, R. (1988) *Yanomamo*, Weinberger

Hart, B. (1993) *Billy The Bus*, Fountain Publications

Hart, B. and O'Gorman, D. (1989) *The Pearlies*, Fountain
  Publications

Hart, B. and O'Gorman, D. (1991) *The Pied Piper of Hamelin*,
  Fountain Publications

Holdstock, J. (1996) *Doobeedy Doo, Four Concert Rounds For
  Juniors*, distributed by Lovely

Marsh, L. (1996) *Song of the Earth*, Piper Publications

Marsh, L. (1988) *Starship 92*, Piper Publications

Marsh, L. (1986) *Along Came Man*, Piper Publications

Christmas

Singing Together, Christmas Collection, BBC

Hart, B. and O'Gorman, D. (1989) *The Late Wise Man*, Fountain
  Publications

Hart, B. and O'Gorman, D. (1992) *The Birds of Christmas Day*,
  Fountain Publications

Marsh, L. (1990) *A Tree of Light*, Piper Publications

Children's books to generate composing

Barber, A. and Bayley, N. (1993) *The Mousehole Cat*, Walker
  Books

Brown, R. (1992) *A Dark, Dark Tale*, Red Fox

DE LA Mare, W. (1986) *The Voice*, poems chosen by Brighton C.,
  Faber

Durant, A. and Parker, A. (1994) *Snake Supper*, Picture Lions

East O' The Sun and West O' The Moon (1991) Walker Books

Inkpen, M. (1995) *Lullaby Hullabaloo*, Hodder

Rosen, M. and Oxenbury, H. (1993) *We're Going On A Bear
  Hunt*, Walker Books

Maddern, E. and Kennaway, A. (1996) *The Rainbow Bird*,
  Frances Lincoln

McAllister, A. and Barrett, A. (1996) *The Ice Palace*,
  Hutchinson

Sendak, M. (1992) *Where the Wild Things Are*, Picture Lions

Sheldon, D. and Blyth, G. (1993) *The Whale's Song*, Red Fox
Sheldon, D. and Blyth, G. (1995) *The Garden*, Red Fox
Souhami, J. (1995) *The Leopard's Drum*, Frances Lincoln
Yickity-yackity yickity-Yak, Poems to Chant, Oxford UP
Wilson, S. (1995) *Good Zap, Little Grog*, Walker Books

Reference books for the library

Eyewitness Music (1989) Dorling Kindersley
Making Music Series (1993) Heinemann
Sharma, E. (1995) *The Ingredients of Music*, Wayland

Special needs

Baxter, K. (1994) *Fundamental Activities* (with video)
     Nottingham: Fundamental Activities
Bean, J. and Oldfield, A. (1991) *The Pied Piper*, Cambridge
     University Press
Birkenshaw-Fleming, L. (1993) *Music For All*, Thompson
     Music, Toronto, Canada
Birkenshaw-Fleming, L. (1982) *Music For Fun, Music For
     Learning*, Holt, Rinehart and Winston
Childs, J. (1996) *Make Music Special*, David Fulton
Wills, P. and Peter, M. (1997) *Music For All*, David Fulton

Posters

Understanding Music
Music around the World 1 & 2 } PCET Wallcharts
Music Timeline
Making Musical Instruments

IT

NCET (1997) *The Music IT Pack* available from NCET, Milburn
     Road, Science Park, Coventry CV4 7JJ (this is aimed at KS3
     but is very relevant to Primary).

Computer software

Rhythm Box, EMR Ltd. 14, Mount Close, Wickford, Essex SS11 8HG

Compose World, ESP. 21, Beech Lane, West Hallam, Ilkeston, Derbyshire DE7 6GP

Rhythm Maker ESP. 21, Beech Lane, West Hallam, Derbyshire DE7 6GP

Music Box, Topologika, Islington Wharf, Penryn, Cornwall TR10 8AT

Notate, Music Studio 32, Longman Logotron, 124 Cambridge Science Park, Milton Road, Cambridge CB4 4ZS

Music Picturebook, IMPAC Resources, Unit 4B, Thornton Industrial Estate, Pickering, N. Yorkshire, YO18 7JB

Capella Software Partners, Oaktree House, Station Rd. Claverdon, Warwickshire CV35 8PE

CD ROMS

Musical Instruments, Microsoft/Dorling Kindersely

Encarta, Microsoft

Peter and the Wolf, IBM

Orchestra, EMI

Music education books

Calouste Gulbenkian Foundation (1988) *The Arts In Schools*

Gardner, H. (1984) *Frames of Mind*, Fontana

Glover, J. and Ward, S. (1993) *Teaching Music in the Primary School*, Cassell

Hargreaves, D. (ed.) (1989) *Children and The Arts*, Open University Press

Hennessy, S. (1995) *Music 7–11: Developing Primary Teaching Skills*, Routledge

Mills, J. (1995) *Music In The Primary School*, Revised Edition CUP

Odam, G. (1995) *The Sounding Symbol — Music Education In Action*, Stanley Thornes

Spruce, G. (ed.) (1996) *Teaching Music*, Routledge

Swanwick, K. (1988) *Music Mind and Education*, Routledge

Instrumental provision and professional musicians in school

Cleave, S. and Dust, K. (1989) *A Sound Start*, NFER-Nelson

Dept. of National Heritage (1996) *Setting The Scene, The Arts And Young People*, Dept. of National Heritage

MANA (1995) *Instrumental Teaching In Context*, MANA

Morely, D. (1991) *Under the Rainbow*, Bloodaxe

Odam, G. (1995) *The Sounding Symbol*, Stanley Thornes

Sharp, C. (1995) *Providing Instrumental Music Tuition — A Handbook for Schools and Services*, NFER

Sharp, C. (1991) *When Every Note Counts*, NFER

Journals

The British Journal of Music Education, Oxford UP

Primary Music Today, Peacock Press

Music Teacher, Rhinegold Publishing

The Music Education Yearbook (Rhinegold) contains a comprensive list of publications, organisations, providers of resources, FE and HE providers of courses and training and other information. Look for it in your central reference library

Funding advice

Arts Council of England
Lottery Department
14, Great Peter Street, London SW1P 3NQ

Arts Council of Northern Ireland
Lottery Unit
185, Stranmillis Road, Belfast BT9 5DU

Arts Council of Wales
Lottery Unit
9, Museum Place, Cardiff CF1 3NX

Scottish Arts Council
Lottery Department
12, Manor Place, Edinburgh EH3 7DD

Association for Business Sponsorship of the Arts (ABSA)
Nutmeg House
60, Gainsford Street
Butlers Wharf, London SE1 2NY
(There are ABSA offices in the regions also)

The Voluntary Arts Network
PO Box 200, Cardiff CF5 1YH

Directory of Grant Making Trusts, 1995

The Handbook of Charities, Frazer Simpson (ed.) 1991

Instruments

The simple message about buying instruments is that, invariably, the more expensive they are the better they sound. The sound quality of an instrument is a direct result of the quality of the materials, design and making. It is a false economy to buy the cheapest instruments as they will not only sound dull, tinny and poorly tuned, but will fall to pieces more quickly.

Visit a music shop which specialises in supplying schools, ask advice from other music teachers and an adviser, visit an education exhibition (inservice courses, summer schools etc. often invite retailers or suppliers to exhibit). Even if, in the end you want to use mail order try to handle and play the instruments first.

Aim for as wide a range of tuned percussion as possible:
(2 or 3 wooden bass bars especially if you regularly work with hearing impaired),
bass xylophone,
alto metallophone and xylophone,
soprano xylophone,
alto and soprano glockenspiels (chromatic if possible),
1.5 octaves chromatic chime bars,
handchimes.

For general classroom work aim for more wood than metal to avoid too much resonance! Most affordable xylophones are no longer made of wood but of a synthetic resin; perfectly satisfactory until you are spoilt by playing a really well made wooden one (a Sonor or Studio 49 bass xylophone costs around £600).

Build up a basic range of wood blocks, shakers, scrapers, bells, drums and a good quality suspended cymbal. Different sizes and materials will provide a wide range of tone colours. Many instruments, which in their original state might be rather fragile for the classroom, have been redesigned using plastics. This is sometimes successful but often creates a sound which is penetrating and intolerably loud for classroom use; again test before you buy. Include instruments from different parts of the world which have not been westernised (retuned) or modernised; such sounds are often more subtle, evocative and stimulate interest in ways that a plastic maraca does not.

Most mail-order companies carry a wide range of good quality instruments but it is worth spending a little time comparing prices.

Book

Cotton, M. (1996) *Agogo to Xylophone*, A&C Black

Manufacturers and Suppliers

Drums and untuned percussion, especially Latin American
Remo Percussion

Tuned percussion
Percussion Plus, The Mill, Great Bowden Rd., Market
    Harborough, Leics. LE16 7DE
Sonor Percussion Instruments, available through LMS, 154,
    Sidwell St., Exeter EX4 6RT
Studio 49, available through Schott and Co. Brunswick Rd.,
    Ashford, Kent TN23 1DX

Instruments from around the world
Knock on Wood, Arch X, Granary Wharf, Leeds LS1 4BR
Acorn Percussion Ltd., Unit 34, Abbey Business Park, Ingate
    Place, London SW8 3NS

Steel pans are very much a 'cottage industry' so you will need to find out through the community arts network or LEA adviser whether there is a local maker.

For good quality instruments from other cultures (e.g. Indian classical instruments) it is advisable to go to a supplier located where there is likely to be serious demand. Again, contact relevant arts organisations for advice.

Audio Equipment
> PZM (Tandy) microphones are sensitive and omni-directional for recording classroom groups or concerts
> Recording tape recorder
> Headphones
> Splitter Box
> Personal recording tape recorder for unobtrusive, 'on the hoof' recording during lessons
> Four-track tape recorder for multi-track recording
> Portable CD and double tape recorder
> CD, cassette recorder, radio and good speakers for hall and/or studio

Organisations of particular relevance to primary music teachers

British Federation of Young Choirs, 37 Frederick St, Loughborough, Leics LE11 3BH

British Kodaly Academy, 11, Cotland Acres, Pendleton Pk, Redhill, Surrey RH1 6JZ

Dalcroze Society, 41a Woodmansterne Rd, Coulsdon, Surrey CR5 2DJ

Federation of Music Services Wheatley House, 12 Lucas Road, High Wycombe, Bucks HP13 6QE (a new organisation for instrumental teaching providers)

Incorporated Society of Musicians, 10 Stratford P1., London W1N 9AE

Music Education Council, 54 Elm Rd, Hale, Altrincham, Cheshire WA15 9QP

Music Publishers Association Ltd., 3rd Floor, Standgate, 18–20 York Bldgs, London WC2N 6JU (for copyright information)

Music for Youth, 4, Blade Mews, Deodar Rd., London SW15 2NN

National Association of Music Educators, 52, Hall Orchard Lane, Frisby-on-the-Wreake, Melton Mowbray, Leics. LE14 2NH

Performing Rights Society, 29–33 Berners Street, London WIP 4AA

Orff Society (UK), 7 Rothesay Av., Richmond, Surrey TW10 5EB

Schools Music Association, 71, Margaret Rd. New Barnet, Herts. EN4 9NT

Voices Foundation, 21, Earls Court Sq. London SW5 9BY

Youth and Music, 28, Charing Cross Rd., London WC2H ODB

Music and SEN

Firebird Trust, 27 Newport, Lincoln LN1 3DN

Music and the Deaf, Brian Jackson Centre, New North Parade, Huddersfield, W. Yorks HD1 5JP

Music Education Advisory Service RNIB, Garrow House, 190 Kensal Rd, London W10 5BT

Sound Sense — The National Community Music Assoc. Riverside House, Rattlesden, Bury St Edmunds, Suffolk IP30 0SF

References

ADAMS, P. (1997) *Sounds Musical*, Oxford: Oxford University Press.

AUBREY, C. (1989) *Consultancy in the United Kingdom: Its Role and Contribution to Educational Change*, London: Falmer Press.

CHILDS, J. (1996) *Make Music Special*, London: David Fulton.

CLEAVE, S. and DUST, K. (1989) *A Sound Start*, Windsor, Bucks: NFER-Nelson.

CORNWALL COUNTY ADVISORY SERVICE (1996) *Curriculum Planning Pack* Cornwall: Cornwall County Council.

COTTON, M. (1996) *Agogo to Xylophone*, London: A&C Black.

DAVIES, B. and ELLISON, L. (1994) *Managing the Effective Primary School*, Harlow: Longman.

DAVIES, L. (1993) *Take Note*, London: BBC.

DEPT. OF NATIONAL HERITAGE (1996) *Setting The Scene, The Arts And Young People*, London: Dept. of National Heritage.

DEVON CURRICULUM ADVICE MUSIC (undated) *Health and Safety in Music Curriculum Activities*, Exeter: Devon County Council.

DEVON CURRICULUM ADVICE (1995) *Planning For Music*, Exeter: Devon County Council.

DfE (1995) *Music in the National Curriculum (England)*, London: HMSO.

DfE AND THE WELSH OFFICE (1995) *Music in the National Curriculum (Wales)*, Cardiff: HMSO.

DRUMMOND, M.J. (1994) *Assessing Children's Learning*, London: David Fulton.

DURRANT, C. and WELCH, G. (1995) *Making Sense of Music*, London: Cassell.

FLYNN, P. (1996) *Listening and Appraising: The Full Picture, Primary Music Today*, Issue 6. Hebden Bridge, W. Yorks: Peacock Press.

GLOVER, J. and WARD, S. (1993) *Teaching Music In the Primary School*, London: Cassell.

HANKE, M. and LEEDHAM, J. (1996) *Alligator Raggedy – Mouth*, London: A&C Black.

HENNESSY, S. (1995) *Music 7–11: Developing Primary Teaching Skills*, London: Routledge.

HENNESSY, S. (1996) *Hymn practice, Primary Music Today*, Issue 3, Hebden Bridge, W. Yorks: Peacock Press.

MANA (1995) *Instrumental Teaching In Context*, Leicestershire: MANA.

MANA (1996) *Notes for Governors*, Leicestershire: MANA.

MacGREGOR, H. (1995) *Listening To Music Elements, 5+*, London: A&C Black.

McNICOL, R. (1992) *Sound Inventions*, Cambridge: CUP.

MILLS, J. (1991) *Music In The Primary School*, Cambridge: CUP.

MILLS, J. (1996) *Ofsted Findings Yamaha Education Supplement* **25**.

MUSIC PUBLISHERS' ASSOC. (1992) *Code of Fair Practice*, London: Music Publishers' Assoc.

NCET (1996) *Primary Music: A Pupil's Entitlement to IT*, Coventry: NCET.

ODAM, G. (1995) *The Sounding Symbol*, Cheltenham: Stanley Thornes.

OFSTED (1995) *Music: A Review of Inspection Findings 1993/4*, London: HMSO.

O'NEILL, S. and BOULTON, M.J. (1996) 'Boys' and girls' preferences for musical instruments: A function of gender?', *Psychology of Music*, **24**.

OXFORDSHIRE QUALITY SCHOOLS ASSOCIATION (1996) *Broad Strands of Progression in Music* (pamphlet).

ROSS, M. and KAMBA, M. (1997) *The State of the Arts*, Exeter: School of Education, University of Exeter.

SCAA (1997) *Expectations In Music at Key Stages 1 and 2*, Middlesex: SCAA.

Schafer, R.M. (1972) *When Words Sing*, London: Universal Edition.

Scottish Office Education Dept (1992) *Curriculum and Assessment: National Guidelines: Expressive Arts 5–14*, Edinburgh: HMSO.

Sharp, C. (1991) *When Every Note Counts*, Windsor, Bucks: NFER.

Sharp, C. (1995) *Providing Instrumental Music Tuition — A Handbook for Schools and Services*, Windsor, Bucks: NFER.

Swanwick, K. (1994) *Musical Knowledge Intuition, Analysis and Music Education*, London: Routledge

Wheway, D. and Paterson, A. (1996) *Music Policy Disk*, Leicestershire: Wheway.

Index

ORDER FORM

Post: *Customer Services Department, Falmer Press, Rankine Road, Basingstoke, Hampshire, RG24 8PR*
Tel: *(01256) 813000* **Fax**: *(01256) 479438*
E-mail: *book.orders@tandf.co.uk*

10% DISCOUNT AND FREE P&P FOR SCHOOLS OR INDIVIDUALS ORDERING THE COMPLETE SET
ORDER YOUR SET NOW. WITH CREDIT CARD PAYMENTS, YOU WON'T BE CHARGED TILL DESPATCH.

TITLE	DUE	ISBN	PRICE	QTY
SUBJECT LEADERS' HANDBOOKS SET		**(RRP £207.20)**	**£185.00**	
Coordinating Science	2/98	0 7507 0688 0	£12.95	
Coordinating Design and Technology	2/98	0 7507 0689 9	£12.95	
Coordinating Maths	2/98	0 7507 0687 2	£12.95	
Coordinating Physical Education	2/98	0 7507 0693 7	£12.95	
Coordinating History	2/98	0 7507 0691 0	£12.95	
Coordinating Music	2/98	0 7507 0694 5	£12.95	
Coordinating Geography	2/98	0 7507 0692 9	£12.95	
Coordinating English at Key Stage 1	4/98	0 7507 0685 6	£12.95	
Coordinating English at Key Stage 2	4/98	0 7507 0686 4	£12.95	
Coordinating IT	4/98	0 7507 0690 2	£12.95	
Coordinating Art	4/98	0 7507 0695 3	£12.95	
Coordinating Religious Education	Late 98	0 7507 0613 9	£12.95	
Management Skills for SEN Coordinators	Late 98	0 7507 0697 X	£12.95	
Building a Whole School Assessment Policy	Late 98	0 7507 0698 8	£12.95	
Curriculum Coordinator and OFSTED Inspection	Late 98	0 7507 0699 6	£12.95	
Coordinating Curriculum in Smaller Primary School	Late 98	0 7507 0700 3	£12.95	

I wish to pay by:

❑ Cheque *(Pay Falmer Press)*
❑ Pro-forma invoice
❑ Credit Card *(Mastercard / Visa / AmEx)*

*Please add p&p	
orders up to £25	*10%*
orders from £25 to £50	*5%*
orders over £50	*free*

Value of Books	
P&P*	
Total	

Card Number _____ *Expiry Date* _____
Signature _____
Name _____ *Title/Position* _____
School _____
Address _____
_____

Postcode _____ *Country* _____
Tel no. _____ *Fax* _____

E-mail _____

❑ If you do not wish to receive further promotional information from the Taylor&Francis Group, please tick box.

All prices are correct at time of going to print but may change without notice

Ref: 1197BFSLAD